A LIFELONG INTEREST

E.H.GOMBRICH

A LIFELONG INTEREST

Conversations on Art and Science with

DIDIER ERIBON

T&H

THAMES AND HUDSON

First published as *Ce que l'image nous dit*
by Editions Adam Biro, Paris, 1991

First published in the United Kingdom in 1993 by
Thames and Hudson Ltd, London

Published in the USA as *Looking for Answers*

Printed and bound in Slovenia

CONTENTS

PREFACE

The conversations printed in this volume extended over the period of some eighteen months when Didier Eribon flew over from Paris with his tape recorder to question me about my work and my views. I came to look forward to his visits because I soon realised that he had made a thorough study of my writings and was genuinely out to clarify obscure points and to enquire about any second thoughts I might have had. The difference in language and background rather helped than hindered this enterprise because it necessitated further explanation. He generally spoke in French and I mostly answered in English, but, when it came to revising the whole transcript, I had in front of me his French translation which I occasionally wished to amend or to supplement. I owe him a real debt of gratitude because in asking me to review my collected writings on art history I discovered to my pleasure that they appeared to cohere more than I had dared to hope. It was he who brought out the continuous strands and helped me to put them in perspective.

It was Didier Eribon also who suggested the title of the French edition, *Ce que l'image nous dit.* Much as I like it, I do not feel that it sounds as natural in English as it sounds in French. I therefore suggested *A Lifelong Interest,* to indicate that this book is meant to focus on my thoughts and activities as a historian of art.

Despite this emphasis it was clear from the outset that the story of my engagement with the visual arts could not be told without the basic facts of my biography. Inevitably, therefore, there would have to be some overlapping with the Autobiographical Sketch with which I prefaced my recent volume of essays, *Topics of Our Time.* The reader must be warned, though, that despite the fact that I conformed with the wish of my English publishers to add a number of illustrations, documenting the transformation of my features in the course of the years, this book is emphatically not a biography. Even less is it intended as a collection of miscellaneous reminiscences. Such a project would have taken me far away from the problems in hand. For however much I may have been absorbed in my academic work, I never allowed it to monopolize my thoughts to the exclusion of other lifelong interests, such as music or nature.

I once wrote a lecture entitled 'Nature and Art as Needs of the Mind',[1] and I put Nature first. Thus when my colleagues would ask me where I was going for my vacations, expecting me to say that I would visit certain collections, monuments and exhibitions, I usually replied that my wife and I were going 'cow-watching'. I remember the passage in Samuel Butler's novel *The Way of All Flesh* where the overwrought hero is advised to go to the zoo and watch pachyderms. I find the sight of ruminating cows on the Alpine meadows even more soothing, not to mention the pleasure awaiting us in the higher altitudes where the shy marmots may be sighted gambolling between the rocks.

Though I left my native Austria in 1936 I have retained my attachment to the beauty of the Alps where, since my school-days, I regularly spent a few weeks walking and even climbing high peaks. The friendship with Richard Bing which I formed in these early days has outlasted the countless tragic events of the subsequent years during which he made a brilliant dual career in the United States as a cardiologist and a creative musician.

There can be few vocations, however, which make it as easy as that of the art historian to combine business with pleasure.

During my lecture trips to European cities, to American universities and even to Japan I was happy to find opportunities of worshipping both at the shrines of nature and of art.

More recently, further opportunities for travel were added when I was invited to accept a variety of honours and awards which allowed me and my wife to fly in comfort to many centres of learning and to meet exceptionally interesting people. But to describe all this would require a very different book.

London, July 1992 E.H. Gombrich

PART ONE

The Double Life of a Historian

1

VIENNA AND MANTUA

You were born in Vienna in 1909. Today there is a sort of myth about pre-1914 Vienna. We have this image of it as an extraordinary cultural, artistic and intellectual capital. I believe you take a more sober view of your native city?

I am essentially a historian, and as a historian I have always fought against the tendency to describe epochs and nations in stereotypes and clichés. I know very well that Vienna has been the victim of the sort of stereotyping that I refuse to accept. Actually, in the case of Vienna we are faced with two or three stereotypes that are mutually contradictory. On the one hand there is the Vienna of operettas, waltzes and *Heurigen* – the new wine. (People used to go out to the suburbs to drink *Heurigen*.) That is a Vienna which is quite outside my experience: I can't waltz, or only very badly, and the only time I drank *Heurigen*, in Grinzing, was when I was showing a party of Swedish tourists round, and I didn't like it.

The other cliché is the intellectual Vienna, the birthplace of every modern movement – from Freud in psychology to Wittgenstein in philosophy, Adolf Loos in architecture and Schoenberg in music.... There is also the idea that all this intellectual vitality in Vienna was in some way connected to the decadence of the Austro-Hungarian Empire. I don't believe it. I don't think we were particularly decadent, nor do I think that

that word can meaningfully be applied to a whole culture. It is true that the Austro-Hungarian Empire died during the First World War, but whether or not its death was inevitable is a difficult question to answer. If Franz Joseph had not lived to such a great age and if he had not blocked any change for such a long time, perhaps the empire could have evolved and survived. But it is pointless for a historian to ponder too much on 'might-have-beens'.

Another thing that is often said is that the Viennese contribution to the modern world was in large part Jewish. That is a considerable oversimplification, and one would have to analyse it at much greater length to establish whether it were true. It is a question, anyway, of no particular interest except to racists, but since it has been raised, it may be useful to remember that Loos was not a Jew, nor was Webern, nor was Berg, nor Klimt, nor Kokoschka, nor Musil, nor Doderer.

You call it a 'cliché', but it seems to me all the same that you were actually part of this mythical Vienna.

Vienna was a big place and was therefore made up of numerous social groups. Some of them got on well together, others hated one another. My family was a typical middle-class family. My father was a lawyer and my mother a pianist. And indeed, although I warned you a moment ago against associating me with the stereotype of Vienna, I have to admit that I did have some contact with that world, at least by proxy, during my childhood as well. My father Karl, who was born in 1874, had been at school with Hugo von Hofmannsthal, the librettist of *Rosenkavalier*, and they were very close when they were young. I still have two letters from Hofmannsthal to my father, showing how highly he regarded him.[2] But later, when Hofmannsthal sided with the aesthetic and symbolist movements and became rather recherché, my father did not like it very much and he gradually moved away. He preferred simplicity.

My father's family came from Germany. My grandfather was born in Offenbach. He was a wholesale dealer in lace; he moved to Vienna and married a girl from Frankfurt. There was a very large and prosperous Jewish community in Frankfurt. As I said, my father was a lawyer. He never enjoyed this job; he would have liked to be a scientist, but it was a strictly patriarchal society and his father had said: 'You will become a lawyer.' And he became a very respected lawyer. He became the vice president of the Disciplinary Council of the Lawyers' Chamber.

My mother was born Leonie Hock, in Vienna in 1873, the youngest of four children. She too was of Jewish extraction, but her father was born in Prague, I think in 1813 or 1815. He came to Vienna and started to work but he was not a good businessman and he was not rich, and he actually went bankrupt in the crash in 1870, so she had a relatively restricted childhood. Her father did not want her to have a Jewish education. He sent her to a non-denominational school, *Das Paedagogium.* So she had no knowledge of the Jewish tradition. My father had some knowledge of this tradition.

And you yourself?

No, I have never been touched by Jewish education.

My mother was attracted to music from the very beginning. She used to tell us how when she was small her father would take her to hear Johann Strauss play in the Volksgarten and she enjoyed playing Viennese waltzes on the piano to the end of her life. I even have a recording of her, made when she was over eighty. Her musical talent was discovered very early, when she went to the conservatoire, where Anton Bruckner was one of her teachers in musical theory. I remember how she used to imitate the very broad Austrian accent in which he explained the laws of harmony. The students often asked him not to go on teaching but to play for them on the organ, and my mother used to work the bellows for him. Later, she went to the famous teacher Leschetitzky, who taught Artur Schnabel. At first he said: 'No, I don't want you, I don't want anybody from Vienna.' But my mother started crying and he said: 'All right, play for me,' and then he took her. She later became his assistant.

She often heard Anton Rubinstein, whose interpretation of Beethoven made a deep impression on her, and she also heard Brahms accompanying a singer at the piano. While she was at the conservatoire she sometimes played with Schoenberg, but she did not like him, either as a musician or as a person. He liked to play the cello in a trio with her and a friend of hers, but she did not enjoy playing with him because, she said, he was no good at keeping time. I asked her, later on, 'Why didn't you become a professional performer?' and she answered: 'My mother would have thought it was as if I wanted to become a circus rider.' At that time, it was not so easy for a girl to 'display' herself in public. So she started teaching, and did not play very often in public.

As a young woman she also knew Sigmund Freud very well, because one of her relations – the husband of a cousin – the famous pediatrician Kassowitz, had got Freud his first job in Vienna. My mother remembered spending several weeks with Freud during the summer holidays, and she was just as much at home in his house in Vienna. But again, I have to say that she didn't like him much, though she always added that he was brilliant at telling Jewish stories.

To have known Schoenberg and Freud, that is quite something!

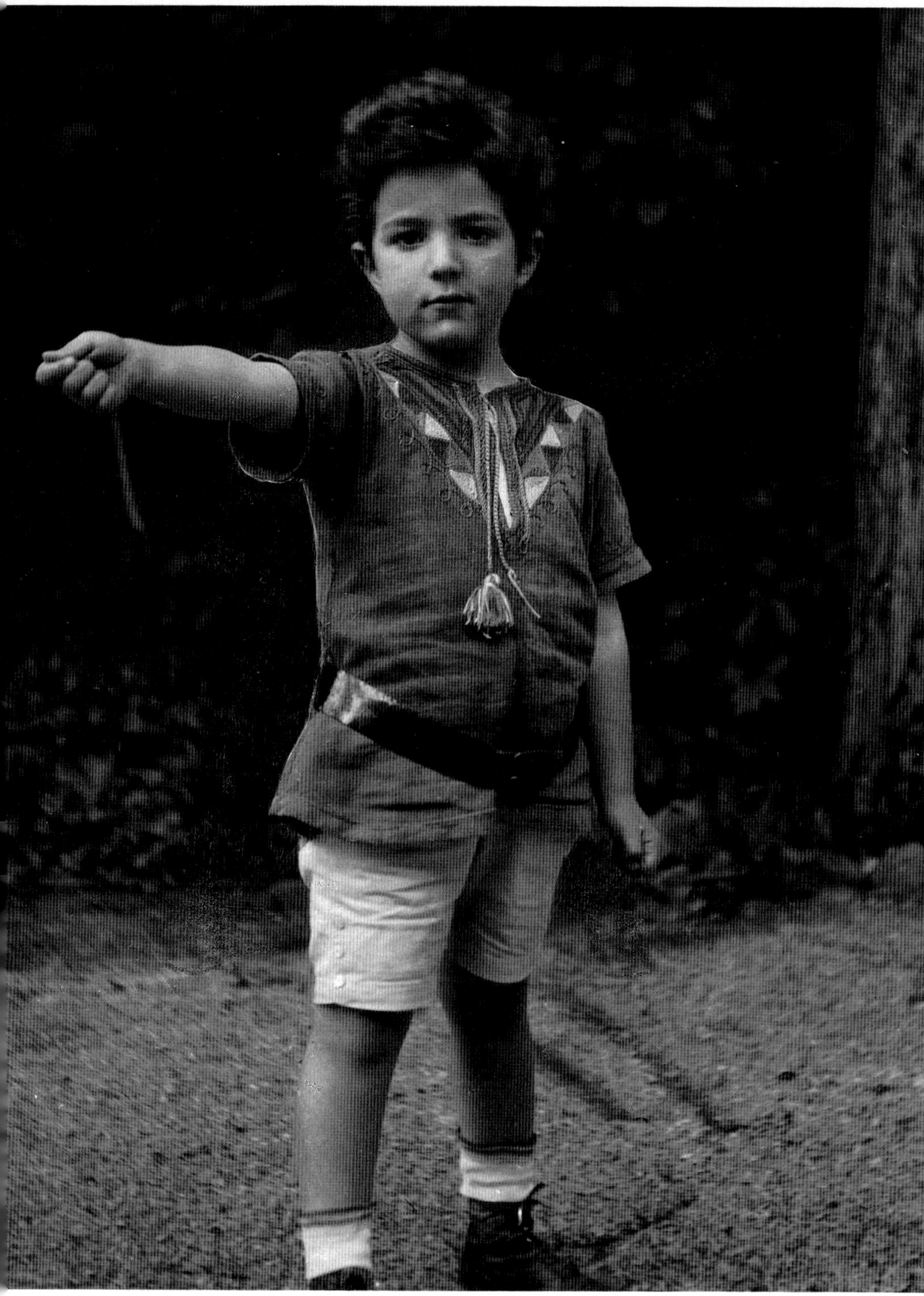

Aged about four, with earthworm

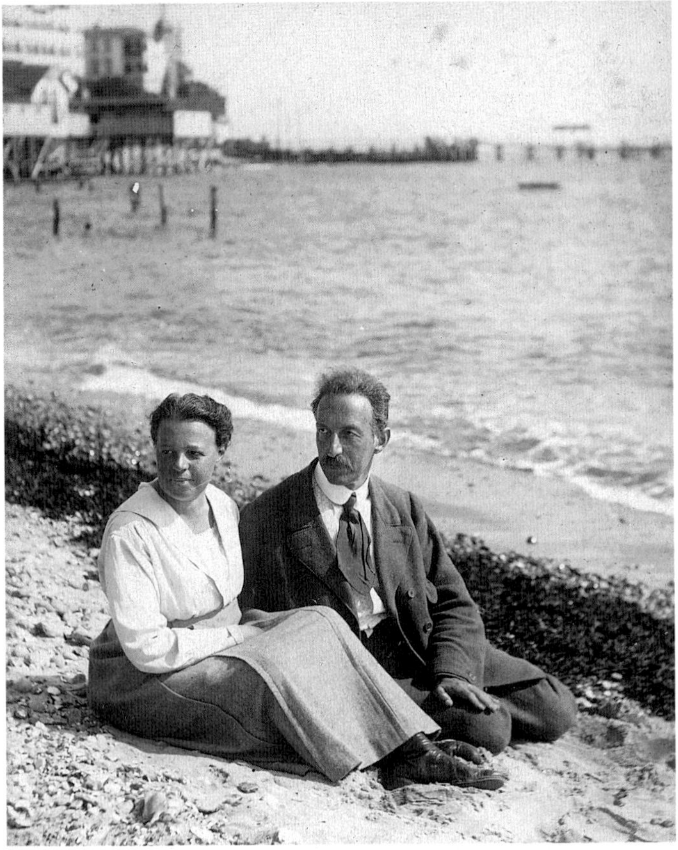

Parents at the seaside, 1921

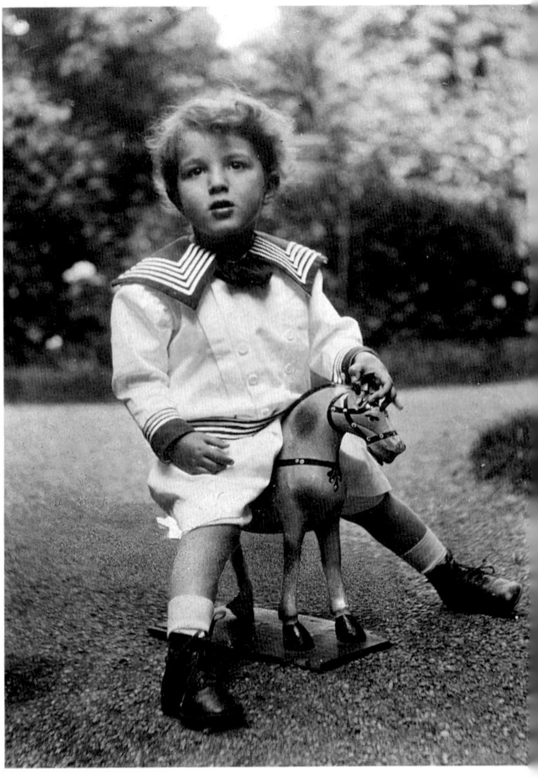

Premonition of the Hobby Horse, aged two

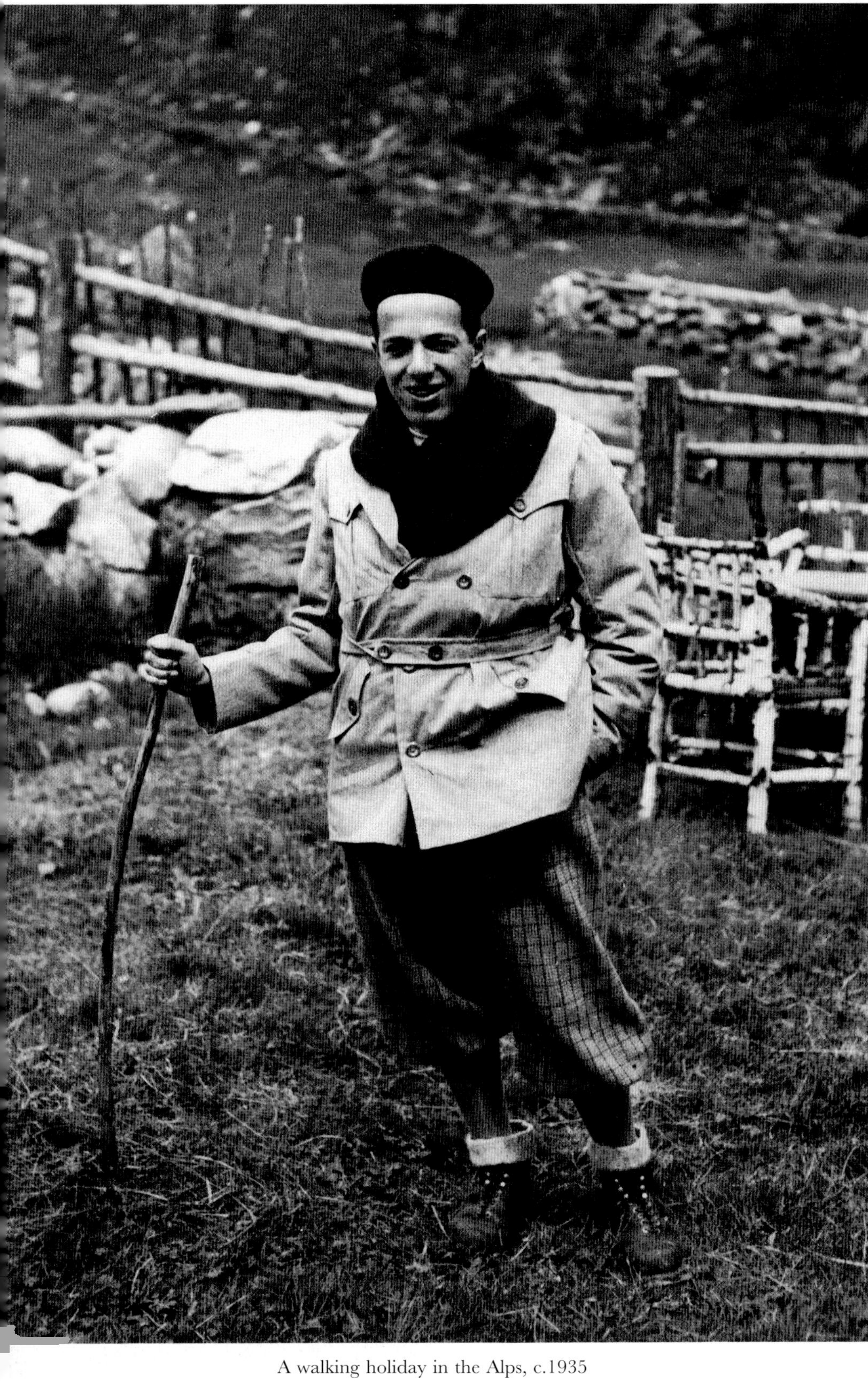

A walking holiday in the Alps, c.1935

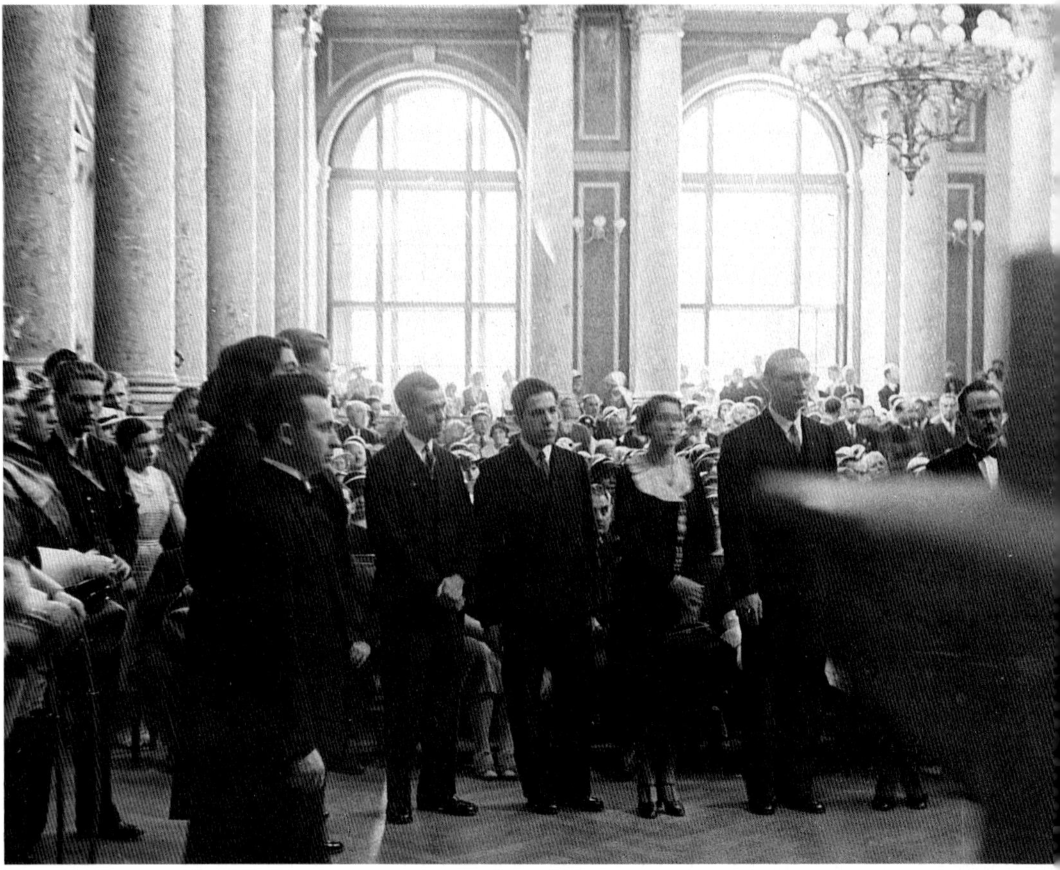

Graduation day at Vienna University, 1933

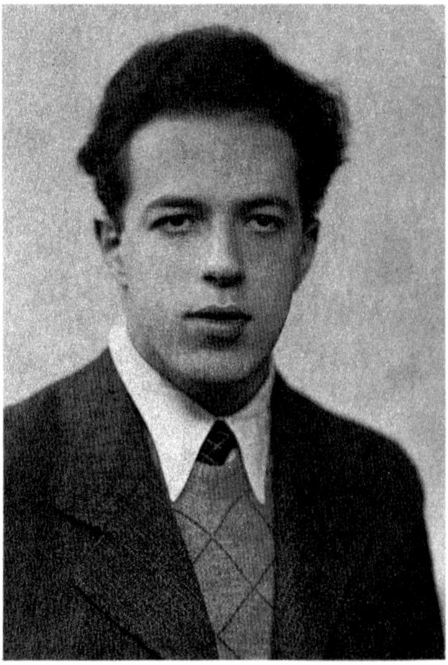

Newly arrived in London, January 1936

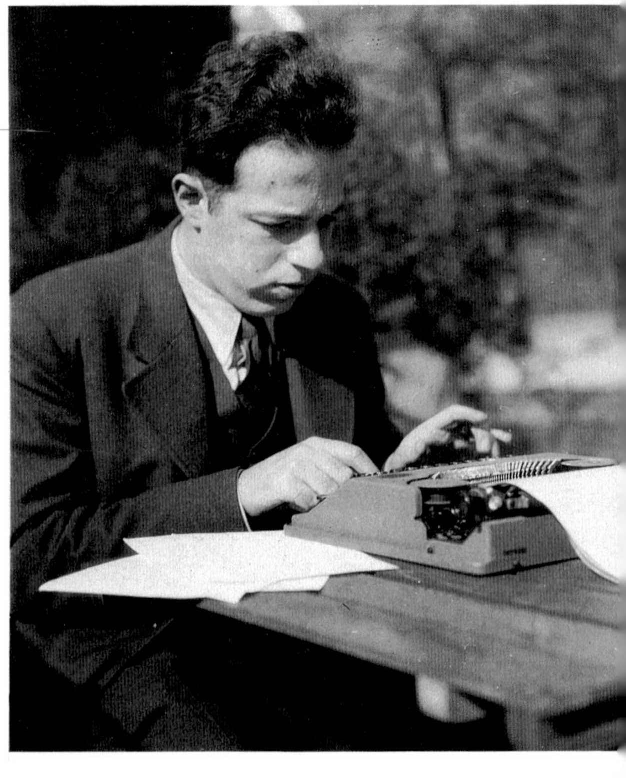

At his typewriter, 1930s

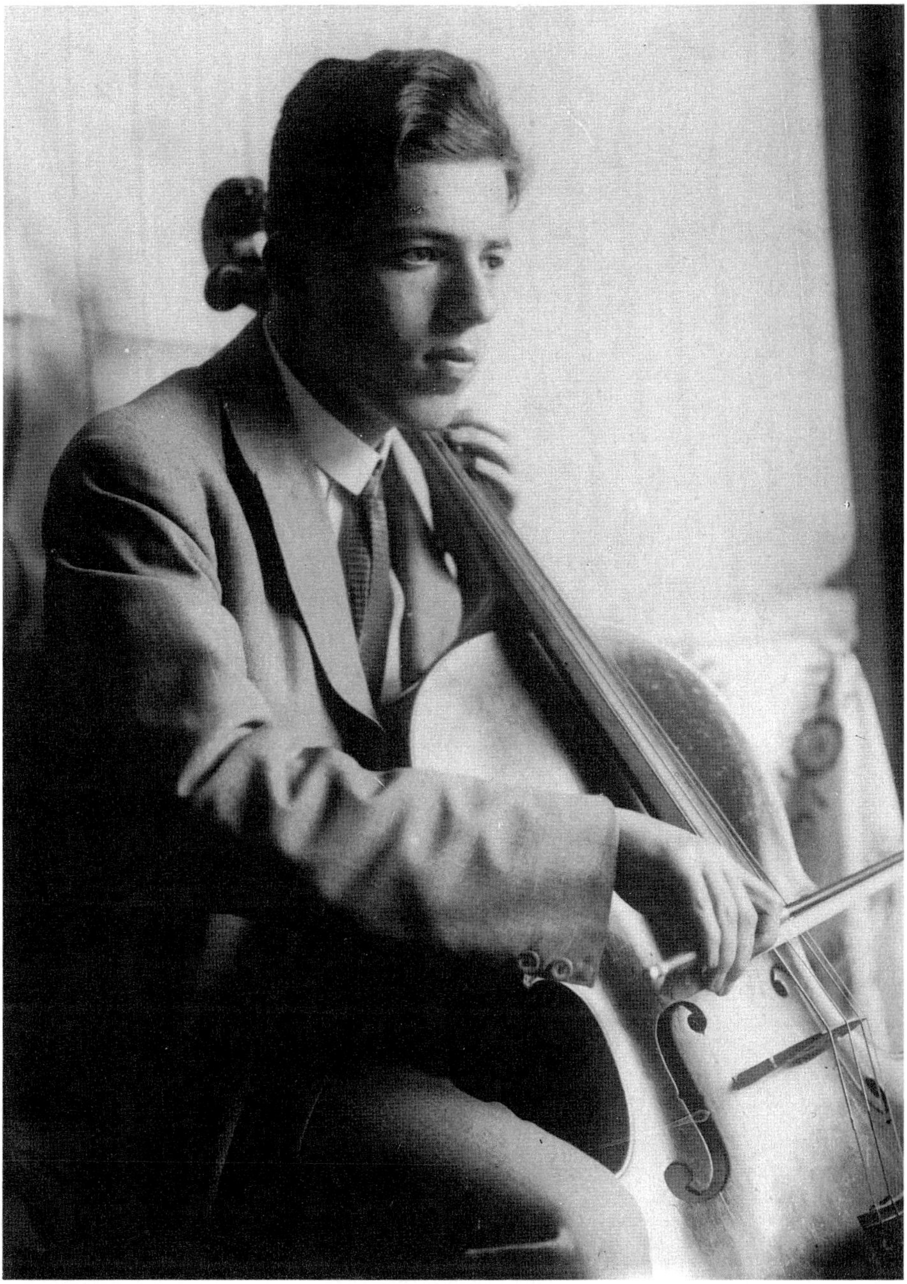

Young cellist, 1930s

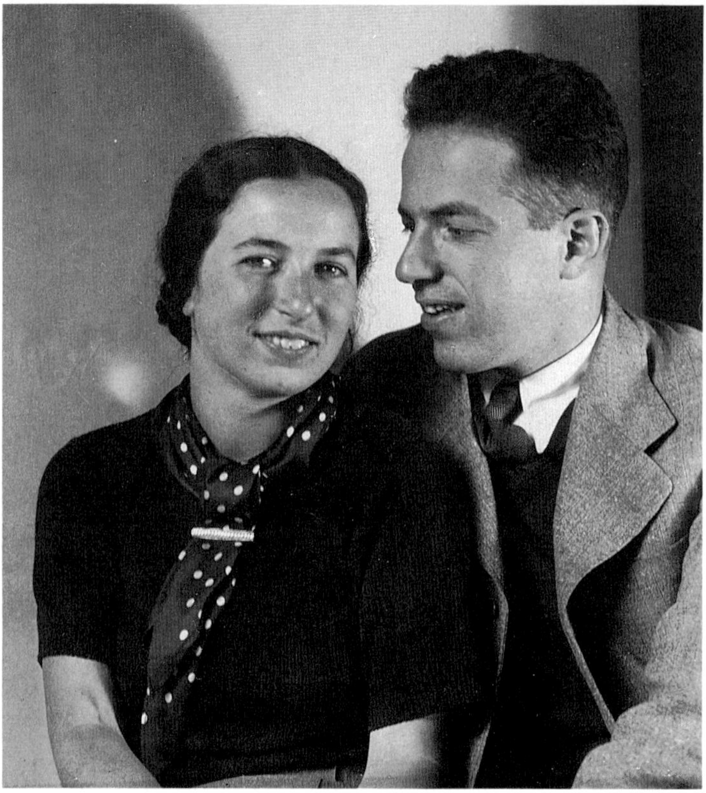

Marriage to Ilse, 1936

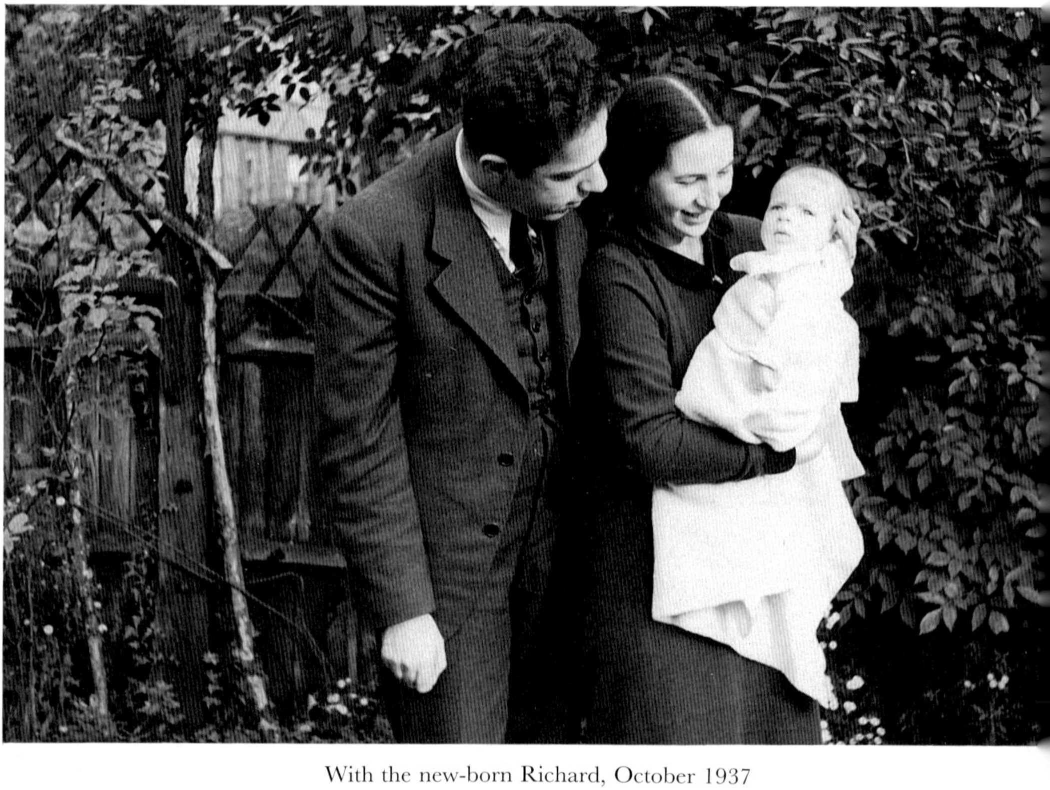

With the new-born Richard, October 1937

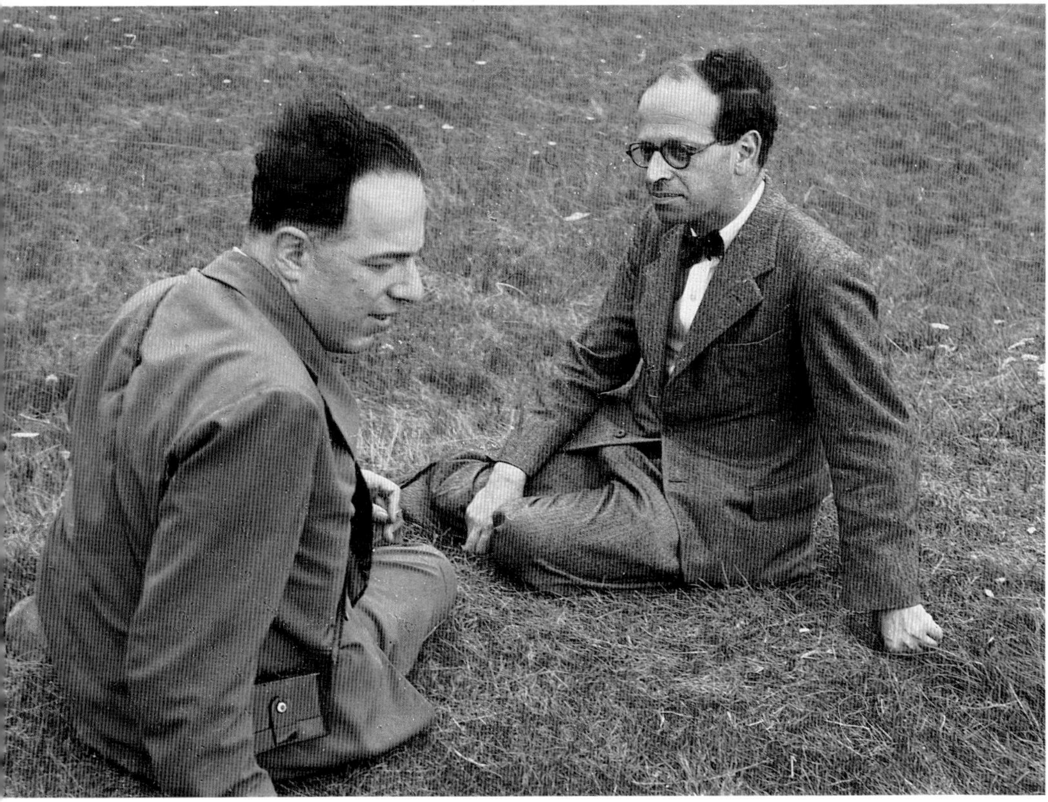

With Leo Ettlinger during the Art Historical Conference in Amsterdam, 1952

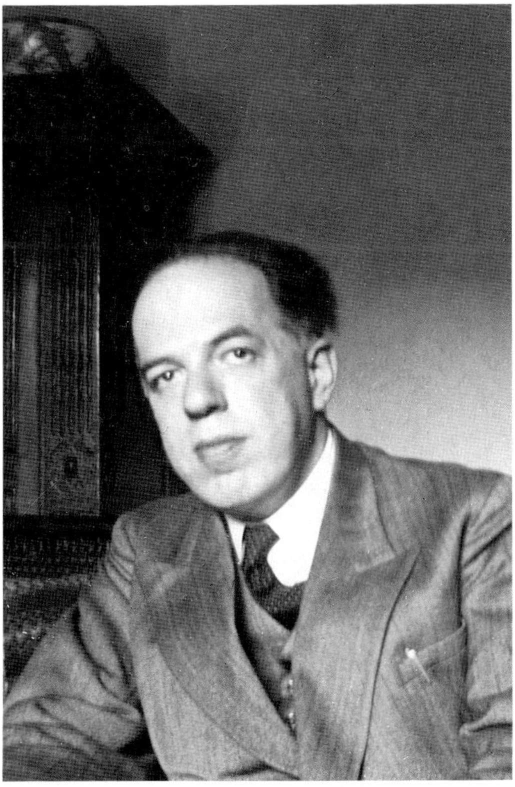

In London in the 50s

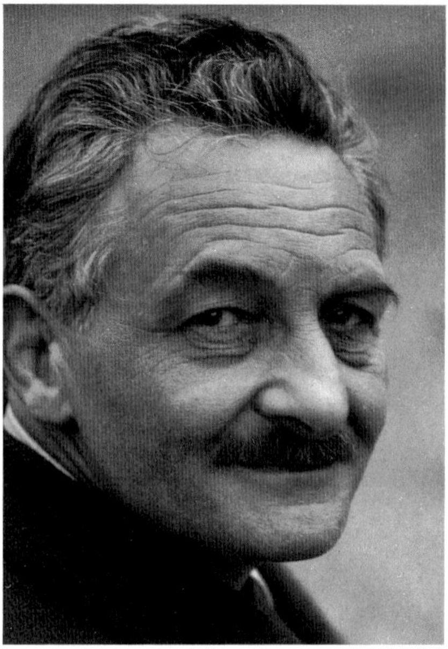

Fritz Saxl

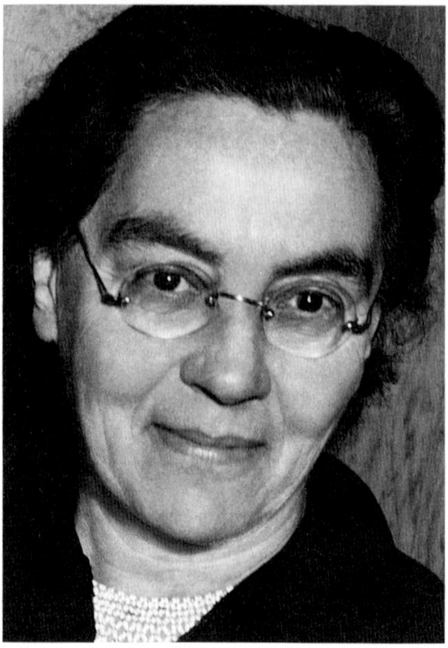

Gertrud Bing

Ernst Kris

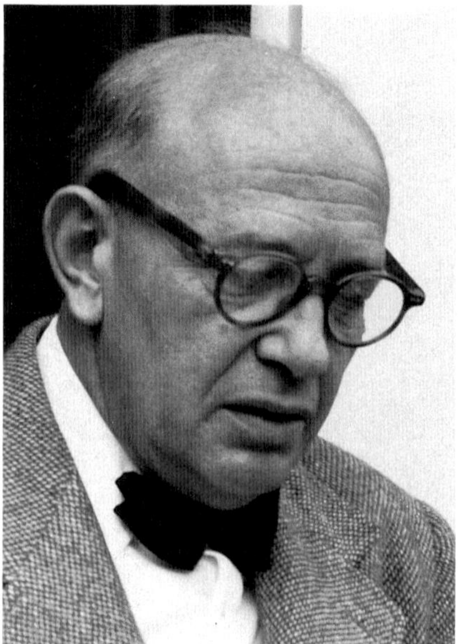

Otto Kurz

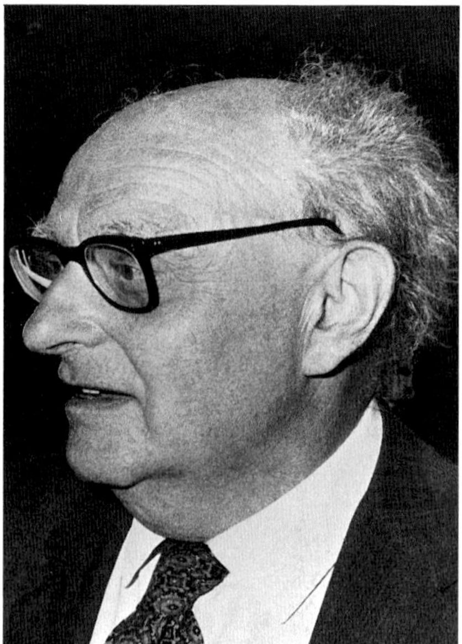

Yes, that's true. And later she moved in the circle of Gustav Mahler, whose sister was her pupil. This was before Mahler married Alma Schindler, but he had already been appointed director of the Vienna Opera and my mother was allowed to attend his rehearsals. This Mahler connection went on in my family. My sister Dea, who became a violinist, was an intimate friend of Mahler's daughter, Anna.

In the Mahler circle, there was a very famous opera singer, called Anna Bahr-Mildenburg, who became an intimate friend of my mother, so intimate that when I was born, and my mother was rather ill after my birth, she invited our family to stay in her villa. So my first few months were spent in the house of Hermann Bahr, who was a very well-known writer and critic.

As you perhaps know, Mahler was very close, in his early years in Vienna, to a philosopher and savant called Siegfried Lipiner. He was a Jew from the east (Poland?) who became a mystical Christian and whose ideas had a great influence on Mahler. Some of his works, like the Resurrection Symphony, were inspired by him.

Lipiner had a circle of admirers who used to go regularly, maybe once a week, to hear him talk about art: he would place a reproduction of an Italian painting on an easel and lecture on it in a style that I think must have been quite like John Ruskin.

He was married at this time to Nina Spiegler, who was much respected by my family and whom I still remember very well. People used to visit her as a sort of pilgrimage, to be granted an audience by her. She also was Jewish by birth but it was she who persuaded my parents to convert from Judaism to Protestantism. Her son Gottfried became one of the first physicists to specialize in radiology. He was one of my closest friends and influenced me very much. It was he who taught me that the interpretation of images poses many problems.

I cannot deny that the Vienna you read about in books did

have some impact on the way I developed, from an early age; but, as I said, the intellectual climate was extremely varied. Then, as now, people were individuals and chose whom they would like or not like and what they would like and not like. But it must be clear, after what I have said, that my contacts with these famous Viennese figures were very largely second-hand.

Even so, they do seem to form a sort of background which must have had its effect on the intellectual atmosphere that formed you.

When I think about it, I have to admit that the atmosphere of Vienna influenced me in a general way: the Viennese middle classes at the beginning of the 20th century attached a great deal of importance to something they called *Bildung*, that is, culture at a general level. I can't deny that there was an element of social snobbery in it, but nobody was taken seriously or accepted socially if they did not take part in this general culture, in music, literature and art. To be ignorant in these areas was to be in a way *blâmable*. It's true that this 'general' culture which one was supposed to have was actually very selective. It included hardly any science and it corresponded to certain intellectual fashions. Russian and Scandinavian writers were very well known – more, I think, than French. My parents did talk quite often about Maupassant and Anatole France, but not about Proust. My mother's two brothers (one was a doctor, one a lawyer) were totally unmusical. But they were immensely learned. They had a fantastic knowledge of the Greek, Latin, French, Italian, and Scandinavian classics, but knew little about practical matters. They naively took it for granted that everybody was as learned as they were.

Beside this value placed on *Bildung*, the middle classes also attached great importance to correct behaviour, to the avoidance of vulgarity in all its forms – and there too there was an element of snobbery. One should remember that the famous satirist Karl Kraus, who figures so largely in evocations of Golden Age Vienna, devoted a great deal of his attention to the correct use of the German language and especially loved to make fun of immigrant Jews, who contributed to newspapers without being completely fluent in German.

In their insistence on being *comme il faut*, the middle classes stressed particularly the avoidance of ostentation, which was considered a mark of the *nouveaux riches*. There are many stories whose point was the ostentation and lack of culture of such people. And one has to add that again it was largely the Jewish immigrants who were the butt of satire. It's true that these middle-class values were not specifically Viennese, but possibly the presence of the Jewish factor in Vienna gave them a distinctive flavour.

So the middle classes, even if they were themselves of Jewish origin, did not welcome the new Jewish immigrants?

No, because they were very anxious to be assimilated into the local traditions and culture of Vienna. And here I cannot agree with some of the things that have been written on this subject. For the simple fact that they wanted to conform to the values and life-style of traditional families shows that there really was a local tradition of high culture among the professional classes and within the Habsburg court circle. It is a culture that Musil and Joseph Roth describe nostalgically in their novels.

I believe that antisemitism was quite virulent in Vienna at this time.

During my childhood and youth, before the Nazi movement really got under way, no one ever inquired whether a friend was Jewish or not. There were many mixed marriages, particularly among intellectuals and artists. Antisemitism was despised as vulgar. I know that the situation was somewhat different in the world of politics, where the conservative party did propagate antisemitism and drove Jewish intellectuals into the socialist and Marxist camp.

As far as I myself am concerned, this early experience has left its mark on me to the extent that it always bothers me when people put the emphasis on race and religion, for I consider all forms of nationalism and chauvinism as unfortunate aberrations. I have not the slightest wish to deny or to conceal my Jewish origins, but when I think of history I think of Western culture rather than the culture of the ghetto, of which I know, perhaps, too little.

Do you still have memories of this period in Vienna?

I was born in 1909. I was the last of my parents' three children. Five years later the outbreak of the First World War put an end to a whole mode of life. One day – this is among my earliest memories – I saw the Emperor Franz Joseph passing in his coach on the way to his palace of Schönbrunn, and I also remember seeing his funeral, which we watched from a window overlooking the Ringstrasse. My memories, as always with very distant memories, consist of a few vivid images: I remember the last white bread rolls that we had for breakfast, because after that white bread was forbidden. I remember also leaflets dropped by the Italians when d'Annunzio flew over Vienna, and I remember the posters saying that if you noticed strange smells, you must immediately report to the police because it could be poison gas. When I was at school, I remember the moment when the teacher rushed into the class with the announcement that a separate peace had been concluded with the Ukraine, and everybody thought that it was wonderful and that the war was over. That was in 1917, I think. I also remember with a certain horror having heard the distant sound of gunfire when we spent the summer of 1918 in Switzerland. It was the artillery of the Italian front, a low, regular booming sound, carried by the wind to the mountain path where we were walking and which I have never forgotten.

I also remember very well the moment when the Austro-Hungarian monarchy broke up, when the revolution happened, in the autumn of 1918, with the collapse of the front. I was nine years old, and we were of course interested in events. I remember very well when this break-up came, when people told us that Bohemia would no longer belong to Austria, the Czechs wanted to be independent, and so on... And I remember the inauguration of the Republic of Austria, which was on the 11th of November 1918. The reason why I remember it very vividly is that it was after all a great moment; there was an enormous cortège on the Ringstrasse, a lot of people, demonstrations with flags and so on, and my parents thought we should go there – it would be a memory for us – but as we came to the Ringstrasse my mother, who had very sensitive ears, heard that there was something wrong a little further on. The regular cheering changed into shouting and she wanted us to turn back. Actually, people started running, because there was a stupid attempt by a small Communist group to fire at the Houses of Parliament. I don't know whether there were any dead, but there was a panic and we ran very fast and reached home.

In his biography of Freud, Peter Gay singles out the food shortages as the thing that people remember about Vienna during and just after the war.[3]

Life was hard, but we were relatively lucky because for medical reasons my father was exempt from military service. But, indeed, when one is talking about Vienna during the war, that is the first thing one should mention: rationing, the difficulty of finding enough to eat. It eventually became so bad that one had to buy on the black market. My father, who was a very law-abiding and moral man, resisted for a long time but in the end he succumbed because there was just nothing. He said that now he was 'joining the society of the semi-decent people'. My mother's elder brother was a doctor, and family doctors were sometimes asked to write certificates so that the children could get milk, but he refused to do it, because, he said, 'You can still afford other things,' and he thought that he should look after the children who were really poor.

After the collapse of the monarchy, the economic situation got even worse. I remember the schools went on strike because one of the teachers had died of starvation. There was an organization, which still exists, called Save the Children, and that tried to help the children of Vienna, and organized that the undernourished children should be sent to Holland and Scandinavia and fed there. I was among those who went. There were five degrees of malnutrition and I got as low as the fourth. So, with my younger sister Lisbeth, we went to Sweden, for nine months. It was just after the war, in 1920. And, as children learn foreign languages very easily, I was soon speaking fluent Swedish (I can still read it, but I don't speak it very well now). My sister lived at the house of a furniture dealer who was also a policeman, and I lived with a cabinetmaker whose main occupation was making coffins. They were very nice people and I hope they cured me a bit of my snobbery. We kept in touch for many years.

But in spite of all the problems of that time, you still managed to begin your education.

At home, my father read very often to us children. And he usually read from Homer. He also read translations of Indian poetry, from the Mahabharata, Nala and Damajanti... So that we had a kind of introduction to various civilizations. Children were not supposed to read everything. Our parents suggested: 'Now you should read this, and now you should read that...' and we did. So there came a moment when my parents thought it was time for me to read the German classics and I started reading Schiller, Goethe, and so on. But, it was all, in a way, within the family circle. We went to the theatre, to the Opera...

We belonged to the middle class but we certainly did not think of ourselves as well off. There were a number of stock-exchange crashes after the war in Vienna. My grandfather lost all his money, and my father lost everything he had saved. (This turned out to be very lucky afterwards because the Nazis would not have allowed him to emigrate so easily had he been rich.) There was no luxury. My mother had an elder sister who became chronically ill and my father had to meet the cost of her living at a home. That was why my mother started giving piano lessons again after the war, as she had done before, because she did not want my father to pay all the cost. So we were very much aware of the fact that money was not easy to earn. But this was not unusual in our circles, because economic circumstances in Vienna were restricted and so no one was wealthy. On the other hand, we were not poor. It may seem now incredible, but everyone had a cook and a parlourmaid, and, as children, we had a nursery maid. And somebody who came for washing, for sewing.... And we went for holidays, to the country, and so on.

What kind of schools did you go to?

My parents thought that I was not very strong, so I went to a very soft primary school, which was a private school. It was here that I had an experience that was very characteristic of the change of régime. The headmistress, a rather silly and pompous woman, had the custom of delivering a loyal address on the emperor's birthday, standing in front of his portrait. She used to say that goodness shone from his face, which even at that age I found a little ridiculous and exaggerated. But the day came when there was no emperor's birthday to celebrate, but the birthday of the republic instead. It was decided that I should recite a poem before the audience about the revolt of the bees. The poem had been chosen because it seemed suitable to the occasion. But, unfortunately, the first line was: 'The queen-bee said, "Throw out the drones." ' When the headmistress realized this, she suggested that it might be better to leave out all references to the queen-bee. I told them this at home and we laughed a great deal. But when the moment came for me to recite the poem I began with the first line before I could stop myself. I remember how embarrassed I was at that point, and how upset the headmistress. So you see, my experience of the transition from a monarchy to a republic was a very concrete one.

While we were in Sweden, my father should have entered me for one of the secondary schools in Vienna, but he left it so late that there were no free places in any of them except the Theresianum. This was founded by Maria-Theresa in the 18th century for sons of the nobility and officers of the army. But after the war it became an ordinary, good Gymnasium. Some of the teachers were very conservative and traditionalist in their ideas, but it was a good classical school and I owe it a great deal.

I can't say I was happy at school. I was rather an outsider, and my classmates soon learned that it was easy to make me lose my temper and that it was fun to see me in a rage. I had a very good memory and was therefore very bored when they were going through things that I knew already. I spent a good deal of my time writing poems about how bored I was. I still have about sixty of these comic poems about the torments of geography lessons and so on. On the other hand, I soon won a certain respect from my teachers. I remember one of them, when I was once again about to give the answer to some question, saying: 'You go into the corner and do knee-jerks instead.' He was tired of my classmates always relying on me to answer all the questions.

A little later I had to choose two main subjects for the oral part of my school-leaving exam. For the first I chose German literature, and for the second physics. I read books on modern physics and on the model of the atom constructed by Niels Bohr. I was trying not to limit myself to a single area of interest. Besides, if one chose German literature (the very essence of *Bildung*), it meant Goethe above all. And Goethe had had a multiplicity of interests: he was interested in science and he aimed to be a universal man. In this respect our system was better than the English one. In England, if you choose science you stop reading literature. And if you opt for literature you lose all contact with science. I am grateful that we did not have this system in Austria. I take the *Scientific American* regularly. I don't understand everything in it, but I am not completely ignorant of scientific progress and particularly scientific method.

But your main interest was in German literature?

Yes, I read Goethe and Schiller. I think I read much more then than I do now. Afterwards I wrote on German literature and I recently collected into one volume a number of essays about German literature that I have published[4]. They are about Goethe, Schiller, Lessing.... I dedicated it to the man who taught me German literature. He was an extraordinary man. He was very learned in philosophy and often spoke to us about Plato, or Schopenhauer. Like many people of that time, he was a Wagnerian. I learned a lot from him.

Were you already interested in art and art history at this time?

In my early schooldays, I was much more interested in natural history. I eagerly collected minerals. There were two museums in Vienna, facing each other; one was the Natural History Museum and the other was the Museum of Art. I went very often to the Natural History Museum: there were minerals, butterflies, and so on, but also prehistoric animals, and I gradually became interested in prehistory. And my sister had a book for children on ancient Egypt, called *The Ancient Wonderland of the Pyramids.* I must have been twelve or thirteen when I read that book with tremendous interest. At that time, I became so absorbed by ancient Egypt that I tried to learn hieroglyphics. And from there, I think I went chronologically, and I became interested in Greek art. I must have been fifteen or sixteen when I wrote a long essay on a Greek vase.

But you did not yet have any contact with painting?

Yes, because in my parents' library there were a lot of books about the great painters, Raphael, Michelangelo, Rembrandt, and so on, and one could see them in the museum. Our father took us, when it rained, to the Museum of Art.

But, perhaps even earlier, I was interested in architecture. I was very interested in the different styles of Vienna's buildings and I made sketches of the various decorative forms.... This was part of my interest: I went through the old streets of Vienna to study the decorative forms of Baroque architecture.

How old were you then?

I was probably fourteen. So when the moment came when we had to prepare for the 'matura' and to write an extended essay to form part of the graduation exam, I chose to make a study of the changing approaches to art from Winckelmann to the present day. And I did that for the teacher of German literature I respected so much. It mainly consisted of quotations. I still have it, and my interest has not changed. I'm still very interested in the changes in the approach to art from Winckelmann to the present day. I'm now writing a book about what I call 'the preference for the primitive', which is, in a way, partly how the Romantics saw Italian art, and all those kinds of things, and this goes back to my years in Vienna when I first read the great art historians.

This is, I think, how I gradually came more to the visual arts. But it was not modern art. What is interesting, and quite strange, is that, relatively, in my milieu, one knew very little of what was happening in modern art. Also, one could not see a lot of modern paintings in Vienna at that time: the Impressionists, of course, but not modern painting.

Modern music was a different matter, and I think that is a very important point. My parents were on very close terms with the violinist Adolf Busch.[5] He was a great follower of Reger, but he did not like atonal music at all. And my mother had never liked Schoenberg, as I said before.

This was not the direction in which our taste went. We were very much steeped in classical music: Bach, Mozart, Beethoven and Schubert. I was never very good at music, though I learned to play the cello a little. But since I married a pianist (a pupil of my mother) music has remained central to my life. I sometimes think I respond more spontaneously to classical music than to the visual arts.

So you were not in touch with the 'Viennese school' which caused such a revolution in musical tradition?

I can't truly say that I was completely out of touch with it because my sister, the violinist whom I mentioned before, got into the circle of Webern, Berg, Schoenberg, and for a time she was very closely connected with that circle.

But to go back to your studies...

By that time, it was pretty obvious that, if I had to choose, it was the history of art. Now I cannot say that my father was very pleased, because he was convinced that an art historian could not make a living. He was quite right. But his father had forced him to be a lawyer and he did not want to force me to be a lawyer too. It was actually pretty hopeless to try to become an art historian, it was a very foolish thing to try, but considering the situation in Vienna, whatever young people tried was pretty hopeless. There was a lot of unemployment, particularly among intellectuals. People could not find jobs. It is one of the reasons why they became so learned.

Your description is very far from the usual clichés about Vienna at this time, for instance, the big Paris exhibition in 1986 called 'La Joyeuse Apocalypse'. [6]

From that exhibition everyone got the idea that the 'Apocalypse' was a very cheerful affair. It wasn't, particularly for the middle classes, who suffered tremendously from the galloping inflation. Because of the inflation, their incomes, their pensions, had disappeared and they did not quite know how to survive at all. So, one must not imagine that the cliché of Vienna being only dancing and music corresponds to the facts I knew when I grew up. It is true that there was a great deal of music in Vienna, and it is also true that the universities were very good. But in the universities there were also many tensions because of antisemitism.

There were clashes between socialists and clericals, and riots and beating of students. The time I spent in Austria was not a happy one. One should not imagine that.

So, in that atmosphere, you went to the university. After having chosen art history.

Yes. There were two chairs of art history and two Institutes. One was Joseph Strzygowski and that was the first Institute. The other was Julius von Schlosser. And by one of those ironies of history, the second was really the first.

Did you have to choose between them?

Yes. And I chose Schlosser. But I went very often to Strzygowski's lectures. It is not really easy to explain. Strzygowski was a very important art historian, in the sense that he was one of the first who refused to concentrate only on Western art. He was interested in the art of Asia, Egypt.... In fact, he was a fanatic opponent of the classical tradition, he hated Roman art, and he thought that only the art of the nomads was creative. He was a bit of a crank. But he had done original work, exploring Armenia, for instance, and many other traditions which had been completely ignored. He was a very interesting man. I know he became a Nazi, but only marginally. He was never an antisemite. I was interested by Strzygowski's lectures but he was so arrogant, so fond of talking about himself and about how important his discoveries were, that I was a little repelled. The lectures were like political rallies, there were hundreds of students.... So after a time, I was sceptical about him. And the alternative was Julius von Schlosser. He was the exact opposite. He was a shy old scholar, and his lectures were a sort of meditation for himself. And he was interested only in the

Classics. He hated Strzygowski, who hated him, of course. And one had to make the choice. I went to Schlosser. He had an assistant, called Svoboda, who had to vet the applicants, and he gave me an essay to write, about the history of an early 18th-century church in Vienna called the Peterskirche. I went to the archives and I wrote a little essay about it, and I was accepted. We were a relatively small group of students – twenty, twenty-five – but we were a very close community.

Schlosser had been director of the department of applied art in the Vienna Museum. He had written very important papers on medieval art and on *la litteratura artistica*, a standard work, which is still a standard work.[7] And so, when one was in his company, one was in the company of a very learned man. And I think I learned enormously from Schlosser. His seminars, unlike his lectures, were very interesting. He remembered objects in the museum which he found interesting but puzzling, and so he would assign one of them to one of his students. That is how I came to write about a medieval pyx. I thought that it was not 6th-century, as it was believed to be, but 9th-century. And he said that I was right and that I should publish my opinion. Later he assigned me to talk about Aloïs Riegl's *Stilfragen*.

What was life in Schlosser's institute like?

Inside the institute we led a very happy life. I say 'inside' because during these years gangs of Nazi students began to go round looking for Jews and beating them up. But that epidemic was still confined to the outside world. We were all friends, we threw ourselves into passionate arguments, we went off together to visit monasteries and art collections in the provinces of Austria, and we had a very good time. Many friendships developed, of course, and some have lasted all my life. I can't mention them all, but I should like to single out Otto Kurz, who was later my colleague at the Warburg Institute.[8] We had a tradition of organizing an annual festivity, to which the teachers were invited and which included all sorts of turns. For three years running I had to write sketches for these occasions, which allowed me to work off my frustrations a little and send up art history and art historians.

What sort of an art historian was Schlosser?

Schlosser was very proud of what he called the Vienna school of art history. You will ask: what is the Vienna school of art history? It can best be defined by looking at something that is almost a foundation document. The first teacher to belong to this school was Franz Wickhoff. Around about 1900 to 1911 he and a few others published a journal called *Kunstgeschichtliche Anzeigen* and there, in the first issue, is a sort of manifesto. This is really a manifesto against amateurism: so much writing on art is fine writing, *belles-lettres* rather than scientific and precise, and we must get away from all this, and what we need are documents… It contained terrible reviews of other people's writings, always condemning them for the slightest inaccuracy and so on… But that was in a way the mission they gave themselves: art history must be taken seriously, as a science. Of course it is not a science, but they thought it was…

And you yourself, did you think it was, at that time?

Of course. I believed that art history must be rational, clear. And that one must not talk any nonsense…. That, I still believe!

Do you consider yourself as the heir of this tradition?

Absolutely. I have called myself so several times. I very much absorbed this tradition in my student years. I think that I can say that I am a member of the Vienna school of art history. And the Vienna school of art history was not all that far from Warburg's. Aby Warburg belonged to a similar generation and had a similar ambition. Schlosser had a very high opinion of Warburg and Warburg a very high opinion of Schlosser. In fact, when Warburg wrote his will, one day in 1905, or whenever it was, he appointed Schlosser his executor.

So it was under Schlosser that you wrote your doctoral thesis on Giulio Romano?

In Vienna at that time the burning question was Mannerism. Everybody was talking about Mannerism. The style had become very fashionable in the early thirties. Up till then, even for Berenson and Wölfflin, Mannerism had been a period of decadence and decline. But in Vienna there had been a strong movement to rehabilitate styles that had been despised. This reappraisal had begun with medieval art. Then Baroque. 'Baroque', you know, was originally an insult; but then, little by little, it came to be seen as something splendid. Mannerism was still thought of as decadent, but in the twenties a small number of people, under the influence of modern art – 'anti-classical' art – began to get interested in it. When Dvořák wrote on El Greco and Mannerism in the early twenties he made an explicit connection between Mannerism and modern art. I could list many books and articles published at that time in which Mannerism was treated in a positive way. The crucial question was to discover what had caused Mannerism, and what it meant to its own time: was it a spiritual crisis? And so on.

As soon as it was decided that Mannerism was a style in its own right, just like the High Renaissance, people stopped calling it 'Late Renaissance' and called it Mannerism. But then another question arose: if it really was a style, like Baroque and Rococo, there must be a Mannerist architecture too. There was a great deal of discussion about this problem. It was just at this moment (the early thirties) that I went to Italy. And, on my way back, I stopped at Mantua and I saw the Palazzo del Tè, built and decorated by Giulio Romano, Raphael's favourite pupil. It was built for Federigo Gonzaga between 1527 and 1532, near his celebrated stables, outside the city walls, to serve not as a residence but as a place for relaxation and festivities. The building still makes a powerful impression by the astonishing variety of the rooms decorated by Giulio Romano and his assistants, with portraits of horses, mythological scenes, and the notorious chamber of horrors, the Room of the Giants. I said to myself: 'Right! Here is a building decorated in what we call the Mannerist style, and the architect is the same person as the painter who did the decorations. So it will be interesting to inquire whether the architectural style is also Mannerist.'

I went to see Schlosser and told him that I wanted to do my thesis on Giulio Romano as an architect. He thought it was an excellent idea. I analysed the architecture and I characterized it as Mannerist. In his architecture Giulio used all those *capriccios* and *jeux d'esprit* which characterized the Mannerist style. My thesis, in which I described both the architecture and the decoration of the various rooms, was published,[9] and it was acknowledged that I had made an important contribution to the definition of Mannerist architecture. At the time I maintained that Giulio Romano had two completely opposed aesthetic languages: one classical and relatively severe, the other extravagantly Mannerist. Today I do not think things are as simple as that, but at the time it made quite an impression. Much later, I realized that I had undoubtedly been influenced by Picasso: Picasso had worked in a Neoclassical style – in his designs for the Ballets Russes, and so on – and he had also carried distortion to an extreme. Thus, an artist could have different modes of expression.

At the time I was a historian of Renaissance architecture. While I was writing my thesis, Rudolf Wittkower, who was working in the same area, simultaneously produced a study of Michelangelo's Laurentian Library, a study in which he reached conclusions that were quite similar to mine. So everyone was in agreement; from now on we should know what Mannerist architecture was.

So that was how I wrote my thesis. It was my apprentice work. I went to the Mantua archives and I got a lot of pleasure from reading the ducal correspondence, and in finding some new documents – not many – on Giulio Romano…

But it was already a real piece of art-historical scholarship.

Yes, I think so. I tried to attribute a few other works to Giulio Romano. My name became associated with him, so much so that when in 1989 there was a great exhibition on Giulio Romano in Mantua I was made the *presidente onorario*. When I arrived all the cameramen were there to film me. It was not the first time I had been there since my thesis. I had become a sort of honorary citizen of Mantua because I had turned the spotlight on the Palazzo del Tè, and that was very good for tourism.

Do you still take an interest in the Palazzo del Tè?

Up to a point. Less seriously than I used to. But I am still interested in it, yes. I liked the 1989 exhibition very much. I wrote a preface for the catalogue on the 'critical heritage' of Giulio Romano, in which I had played a certain part myself.

After your thesis you published another book, but that one had nothing to do with the history of art.

I was awarded my doctorate after five years at the university, which was more or less normal in Vienna, and I realized, without too much surprise, that I was not qualified to earn a living. I gave a few public lectures and I became pretty well acquainted with the disappointments of looking for work. At this point, a publisher I knew, Walter Neurath, was launching a series called *Wissenschaft für Kinder* (Knowledge for Children) and he asked me to translate from the English a history of the world for children. I looked at the book, and I found it so unbelievably awful that I said I would rather write the book myself than translate such a load of rubbish. Naturally, he asked me to write a sample chapter, and I chose the age of chivalry. I wrote a very colourful piece of narrative. I knew what I wanted to do because a short while before I had much enjoyed writing long letters to the daughter of some close friends, in which I told the story of my thesis in the form of a fairy story about a prince who built a beautiful palace. My chapter was approved by the publisher, but he now insisted that I should deliver the complete manuscript in six weeks. That seemed to me impossible but I was intrigued by the challenge. I had never studied history, but I knew that I could find all the facts I needed in the big encyclopaedia we had at home. I felt also that I should give my narrative a certain flavour of authenticity, and so I made it a rule to look for texts belonging to the periods I was writing about, and to include quotations from them at the relevant points. I made myself write a chapter a day, so it was all ready by the appointed date. A former riding instructor who was out of a job was taken on to draw the illustrations. He was not bad at horses; less successful with people.

When the book was published, it was highly acclaimed and soon translated into Polish, Dutch and the three Scandinavian languages. I think it owed its merits partly to the way it was written in such a mad rush and also to the conviction that I had (and still have) that it should be possible to explain anything in language that can be understood by a child. Exactly fifty years later the book was republished in Germany, and it is still selling very well.[10]

It was during these years that you embarked on another work – that was with the psychoanalyst Ernst Kris, whose influence on you and your work has been very important.

Yes, he has been a very important element in my life. Kris was nine years older than me. He was a very unusual man, curator of the Habsburg collection of goldsmith-work in the Vienna Museum. He was a great specialist. In a way, he was an international authority, but he became a little bored with his expertise. His wife, Marianne Rie, was the daughter of one of Sigmund Freud's best friends, Oskar Rie, who used to play cards every week with Freud. Marianne came from that intimate circle of Freud, and when she married Kris, he became part of that circle too. Freud was obviously very interested in this lively man and Kris became an editor of the journal of the psychoanalysts in Vienna called *Imago*, which tried to be not too specialized, but to show how psychoanalysis was applicable to daily life and to other disciplines. And it was this which really became his overriding interest. But to earn his living, and because it was his job, he continued with immense industry to work for the museum in Vienna. He went there in the morning and worked till closing time. Then he went back home and saw patients. Before nine o'clock and after six, he was a psychoanalyst treating patients. This was after he had been trained, of course. He thought for a time of studying medicine and becoming a fully qualified psychoanalyst. But Freud dissuaded him from doing that, as he did all his disciples.

What I really learned from him was that one can combine an

interest in the history of art with interests in more general questions. And he was always imaginative in his general theories and he would try them out in conversation. He used to sketch them out and the next day he would say: 'That was all nonsense.' But this was very stimulating. He was a tremendous reader. He read many things, not only in art history or psychoanalysis, but also in literature. And for me contact with him was very important.[11]

How did you meet him?

He was also a student of Julius von Schlosser who had a great regard for him. He compiled the index of Schlosser's great book, *Kunstliteratur*, and he was very close to him. The first time Schlosser asked me to go and see him was in connection with my article on the medieval pyx that I mentioned. In order to have it taken out of the showcase one had to ask Dr Kris, who kept the key. I went to see him, he took it out and put it on a table, and said: 'Why are you doing this? We know everything about this object. It is not interesting.' He was very dismissive. I have already mentioned the comic sketches that I used to write every year for the students' party. In one of these sketches, which was a sort of imitation Baroque allegory, I showed a young historian being tempted by Doubt, and Doubt was represented by Kris because he was so sceptical about art history by then. I put into verse, in stately German alexandrines, what he had told me when I first went to see him. He was sitting in the audience and I asked him: 'Did you recognize yourself?' 'Yes, I certainly did,' he replied, 'I only hope the others didn't.' And then he said: 'Why are you really studying art history when you can write plays like that?' That was how I came to know Kris.

I gave two papers about this time, one after another, on medieval ivories, and one was published immediately.[12] I soon got to know Kris a little better. At that time he was writing a very interesting paper on Messerschmidt, the Austrian sculptor who was insane and who made a number of physiognomic studies partly derived from physiognomic tradition and partly from his mental abnormality.[13] Kris became interested in the typical kind of anecdote that is told about artists, because in the case of Messerschmidt there was a sort of ficticious biography of such anecdotes in circulation.

Kris had suggested to Otto Kurz, who, as I mentioned, was my best friend as a student, that he should assist him in collecting material for this study of the myth of the artist. (The book has been published again in English with a preface by myself).[14] After that Kris managed to get a job for Kurz at the Warburg Institute, which was then still in Hamburg, and he asked me whether I would take over Kurz's position as his assistant. He had another project in hand, a book about caricature. So I began to work on caricature, with Kris. That was after my doctoral thesis. I spent my time collecting material and reading a lot of 18th-century authors, and we started writing together. Kris was interested in caricature because Freud had written a book on jokes and Kris thought that caricature formed an interesting parallel in art – a joke of a special kind to which one should be able to apply Freud's theory.

So you started writing the book with Kris?

Yes, we wrote it together. Kris was in close contact with the Warburg Institute – which in 1933 had just moved from Hamburg to London, to escape the rise of the Nazis – and with Fritz Saxl, who had taken over as director when Aby Warburg died in 1929.

Kris met Saxl when he visited Vienna, and told him of me: 'I have a young man whom you ought to take for the Warburg Institute.' He was convinced that the Nazis would come to power. The situation was obviously getting impossible. So I met Saxl in a café, with Kris. Saxl wrote to his assistant, Gertrud Bing, that he had found a young man who could help in preparing Aby Warburg's papers for publication.

There is an amusing story behind this. A little earlier than that meeting with Saxl, when Kurz had just emigrated to London in order to go on working at the Warburg Institute, he had lent to me a thriller, a detective story, called *Marco Polo's Millions*, by Frank Heller. (Marco Polo, you will remember, was nicknamed Marco Millione.) Now, when Kurz arrived in London, he found that everybody at the Warburg Institute, which had just arrived there, was expected to work on Marco Polo, because Sir Percival David, a rich collector of Chinese art, had become very interested in Marco Polo and all that, and was looking for experts and historians who could help him publish an edition of Marco Polo's narrative of his travels. So Kurz was amused by all this excitement and remembered that thriller and wrote to me: 'Could you send me back *Marco Polo's Millions*?' So I took it to the post office. The address he had given me was 'Care of Gertrud Bing, at the Warburg Institute'. When I wrote the address, just for a joke I imitated his handwriting. The parcel arrived in London and the librarian of the Warburg Institute looked at it and was convinced that the address had been written by Otto Kurz. But how could he send a parcel from Vienna when he was here in London? As soon as Kurz saw it, he said at once: 'I didn't write this address. It is my friend Gombrich faking my handwriting.'

Well, you know what people are like: this was shown round the Warburg Institute – 'Do you know who wrote this?' – 'Kurz.' – 'No, Gombrich...' and so on. Gertrud Bing was also very amused. She sent me a letter saying how amazed she had been that I could forge Kurz's handwriting so well, and that she now expected me to write her a letter back in her own handwriting. Which of course I couldn't do, but I sent a little poem written in a barely tolerable imitation of her hand, explaining that it had been Sympathy that had guided my hand in tracing the familiar forms of my old friend's peculiar script, but that the severe architecture of her writing was wholly defeating me.

Hence, when in the autumn of 1935, Saxl asked her if he should engage me, she obviously agreed very readily.

This all happened in the autumn of 1935. I left Vienna after Christmas 1935, and spent a few days in Paris. It was the first time I had been to Paris. I saw the Louvre. And I met Charles Sterling, a famous art historian to whom I had been recommended by Kris. I arrived in London in January 1936. Saxl sent a student to collect me at the station. London was very uncomfortable. And of course the Warburg Institute did not pay very well. It was a fellowship for two years, not a permanent post.

Can you say something about the Warburg Institute?

The Warburg Institute (which is now part of the University of London) originated in the library assembled over many years by the great Renaissance scholar Aby Warburg (1866-1929) in his native city of Hamburg. At first Aby Warburg's interest centred on the art and civilization of Florence in the time of Lorenzo de' Medici. In studying the works of Botticelli and Ghirlandaio, he paid particular attention to their social context (in Taine's sense), and he soon found that in order to answer the question to which he had devoted his life – what did the recovery of classical Antiquity really mean for the Renaissance, both positively and negatively? – he was having to buy books on a whole variety of other subjects: on economic history, on religious movements, on philosophy, on the humanists, etc. Thus after the 1914-18 War his library became a research tool for cultural history and quickly gained an international reputation. Then it was transformed into an institute, which worked closely with the newly founded University of Hamburg.

As a Jewish foundation, the Warburg Institute was under threat from the Nazis, who came to power in 1933, and towards the end of that year it migrated to London, lock, stock and barrel.[15] So I found myself once more among very learned men and women, who knew far more about ancient Greece and Rome than about modern England.

2

LONDON

What was the situation at the Warburg Institute when you joined it?

It was very strange, because the Warburg Institute had just arrived in London, and the people then did not know English very well. It was a little chaotic, as you can imagine. A rich man called Lord Mond had made available the basement of Thames House, a building on the embankment, to hold the books and the Warburg had the use of a few rooms.

What did your work consist of?

I was only asked to work on Warburg's papers. When I saw the papers and the photographs, I was horrified. His handwriting was difficult to decipher, and he was a man who never threw anything away, so there were piles and piles of notes and drafts which he started and started again and again. He was very neurotic. But anyhow, I did my best and I even started writing commentaries in English, on his project called *Mnemosyne*, where he had the idea of bringing together many hundreds of photographs in order to illustrate the history of art and culture from his own idiosyncratic point of view. As I was trying to learn English, I started to write directly in English. But Kris and I had not yet finished our book on caricature. Saxl gave me permission, in the summer, to go back to Vienna and finish the book.

Kris was to dedicate it to the Warburg Institute and Saxl was very interested. Meanwhile, during that period of 1936, I also married. My wife complained that we had no time for a proper honeymoon. We just went to Prague for three days to visit her relatives. But Kris and I wanted to finish the book as quickly as possible. We finished it and sent it in a parcel to London. The rest of the story is not very pleasant. Saxl was a very busy man and a sceptical man, and he did not properly read it. He gave it to somebody else to read, who was against psychoanalysis.... So it was never published. And it remains unpublished! We published only an article.[16] But this fat book has never been published.

A pity.

Yes it is, in a way, a pity because it contained a lot of material, not only on caricature but on satire and other such things. But it would make no sense to publish it now because it would be completely obsolete. Kris had this psychoanalytic idea that caricature really was a replacement, a development of image magic.

Much later, just before the war broke out, I was asked to write a little popular book on caricature for Penguin. There is a small bibliographical point to be mentioned here. I wrote the text, but before it came out, I wanted to show it to Kris. This was difficult, because the Nazis were in Vienna.... Yet, although I wrote it alone, the book really had two authors. So, when I came to write the title page, with 'Ernst Gombrich and Ernst Kris' on it, I thought there were too many 'Ernsts' so I called myself E.H. Gombrich, and that is how I am still called.

And this one, this book for Penguin, was published?

Oh, yes, in 1940. It is only a little book but it summarized our theories on caricature.[17]

Could you give us a summary of your thesis?

Freud considered wit to be a channel for aggression, a conscious way of expressing unconscious forces. In the same way, Kris saw satirical drawing as an outlet for aggressive impulses.

He wanted to explore the history of caricature, and especially to trace satirical images back to the practice of black magic. It is evident that imagery plays a role in rituals where a wax doll is used as a substitute for the intended victim and is pierced with pins. Kris was struck by the resemblance between this act of hostility and the custom of hanging or burning someone in effigy, that is, inflicting the death penalty on the image of your enemy. He was particularly interested in the 'defamatory images' of the late Middle Ages. But one has to point out that these insulting images did not involve any distortion of the person's physiognomy. And it is precisely in this difference (between, on the one hand, the aggressive use of an image and, on the other, the artistic medium of caricature) that Kris looked for the explanation of why caricature had appeared so relatively late. As long as aggressive images were, he argued, a form of black magic, it was inconceivable to make fun of some important person's appearance, as Bernini did with the face of the Pope. In other words, as long as people were afraid of magic, the idea of transforming someone's image was literally 'no joke'. So caricature could not come into being until magic had disappeared. And for Kris, caricature replaced image-magic.

You no longer hold that theory today?

No, certainly not.[18] Kris, like Freud, and like Aby Warburg, was completely under the spell of an evolutionist interpretation of human history, imagined as a slow advance from primitive irrationality to the triumph of reason. And just as Warburg had arranged his library in a way that reflected human progress from magic to reason, so our book viewed the history of satire as an analogous development over the centuries. We can no longer see things like that. Too many things have happened to destroy that rosy optimism.

In 'Art and Illusion' you came back to the problem of caricature, but in a wider context.[19]

Yes, I tried to fit the invention of caricature into the more general development of representational art. But I considered it as a technical innovation rather than as a symptom of a change in human consciousness. No one can deny that we have made enormous technical advances, but it is also true that in other ways we are still savages.

When you started to work on Aby Warburg's papers in London, was it intended that you would eventually write a biography of him?

No, I certainly was not expected to write a book! Gertrud Bing, who had been Warburg's assistant, only wanted certain things of his to be published. Warburg's 'collected works' had already been launched in Germany, but it was just before the Nazis took power. Six volumes were planned, but because the Institute moved to London, the plan did not materialize. Saxl thought that we ought to honour the original promise. But it has still not been honoured.[20]

My work was interrupted by the war. Afterwards I returned to the task, but I found that it was not possible to simply publish these papers because they were too fragmentary. I should have had to write a commentary. So I compiled an account of Warburg's ideas, based on his papers. The intention was then that my book should be the second volume of a biography of

Warburg. Bing would write about the life and I should write about his ideas. But Bing died. So I combined the two and wrote the biography myself. It is not really his life story. It is an intellectual biography.[21]

When you came to live in London, was that your only occupation: trying to make something out of Aby Warburg's papers?

No. The rich man whom I mentioned, who had allowed the Warburg Institute to use rooms in Thames House, now said that he needed the space, so the Institute found itself homeless again. All the books had to be packed up. There was no easy way for me to get access to Warburg's papers. So for a time, around the beginning of 1937, I had to do other things. I went into teaching. The Courtauld Institute needed staff and I gave a weekly class for two years, in 1938 and 1939, on Vasari.

At that time the Courtauld Institute was new and as there were no textbooks on art history its director thought that Otto Kurz and I should write one on iconography. We spent a good deal of time compiling a bibliography and writing chapters. I used to read in the reading room of the British Museum.

Did you finish that book?

The book was more or less finished, but it was never published because the war broke out. It consisted of detailed bibliographies arranged under categories like emblems, still life, allegory, mythology, and so on. (I learned a lot compiling those bibliographies, but now, of course, after fifty years, they would be completely out of date.) I also wrote short texts, to give examples of each of these categories. Later I published a few – in fact, most – of these examples. For mythology, for instance, I had chosen the *Orion* of Poussin (now in the Metropolitan Museum, New York).

I discovered in the course of my research that Poussin had used a work by Natalis Comes and had illustrated the explanation that this author gives of the myth as referring to a cloud. That chance discovery actually provided an important insight into Poussin's treatment of myth, which was later followed up by Anthony Blunt and others. I published it as a separate article in the *Burlington Magazine* and reprinted it in *Symbolic Images*.[22]

In a more general way, what did coming to live in England mean for you?

We had several friends here who had been taught by my mother in Vienna. So we knew a few people. But on the whole, the Warburg Institute was rather isolated. Most of us talked German and did not know much English.

So you were not influenced by English culture, and particularly by the more positivist, empirical approach to the writing of history and art history that prevailed in English universities?

I was not at all influenced at that time. We were very isolated. It was an enclave of German and Austrian culture. Saxl tried to make contacts, and he succeeded to some extent, but for us young people there were not so many. It is true that later, a few English students came to the Warburg, but it was not real integration.

You said that the Warburg had to close down for a while and then to move. Where did it move to?

It is an amusing story. The university was entitled to use rooms in the Imperial Institute in South Kensington. And permission was now given for the books of the Warburg Institute to go to the university premises in South Kensington. But there were no bookshelves. So what to do? The building was in the care of the Office of Works, and one of the top civil servants there, Frederic Raby, had to authorise the delivery of the shelves. And he never did anything. For months and months we sent letters to him with no result. It so happened that Raby was not only a top civil servant but also a great scholar (something that could not happen now). His field was Latin poetry in the Middle Ages. He had published two volumes on the subject as well as *The Oxford Book of Mediaeval Latin Verse*.

One day, Kurz said: 'Of course he does not answer letters, he only understands medieval Latin poetry.' So Saxl rang me up one morning, and said: 'Gombrich, you must write a medieval Latin poem.' And so I did one in the style of the 'Wandering Scholars'. Raby immediately wrote back a poem in the same metre, using the same rhyme-scheme, to tell us that we could have the shelves.[23]

But otherwise, things were not very funny. Hitler had occupied Vienna. We were all very, very worried about our relations and friends. It was very difficult to help them to come to England, because one was not allowed to take a paid job unless the employer could prove that he could find nobody in England to do the same work. For me it was not very difficult: the Warburg Institute could easily prove that no Englishman could edit Warburg's papers. I got this permission. But otherwise, it was very difficult. The frontiers were closed, and only if one got a guarantee by an Englishman that one would not have to be supported by the state and the taxpayer could one come. We spent a lot of time looking for people who were ready to sign. The year after the Anschluss, which happened in March 1938, was very terrible for all of us. My parents had not thought of emigrating. They did not see why they should. My father was a respected lawyer and he had no idea that he was really in danger. But luckily (if I can say that) my mother was called to the

Gestapo to be questioned about one of her students. Nothing happened to her, but it made my parents think that it was probably dangerous to stay, and they decided to leave. A family friend of one of my mother's English pupils offered to sign the guarantee. So they came to England. But of course we had next to no money. Life was difficult. One knew that the war was coming. It was very depressing, so much so that I have a slightly confused memory of that time. So many people were in a similar situation.

And then the war broke out.

Most people in England, understandably of course, did not want to go to war. I remember a conversation when Hitler occupied the Rhineland, and a nice lady said: 'Why shouldn't he go there, it's his country.' They did not see the danger. They did not know very much about Hitler. So that was a very tense situation for us. Had Hitler not started the war, the British would never have started it, of course. And so one was in this situation with a terrible life going on back in Austria, trying to find help for people who were in danger, and at the same time going on with one's work. On top of which, we now had a small son. My parents came. My mother immediately started giving lessons. My father, of course, could not find work as a lawyer, and he became a typist in the firm which had brought over their furniture. Yes, they brought their furniture with them! And then, in the end, the war did break out. There were two stages. First, in 1938, there was the Munich crisis, when everybody expected the war to break out. Chamberlain yielded to Hitler's blackmail and gave him the Sudetenland. At that time, when one spoke of the coming war, one thought mainly of bombs and bombing. We expected that on the day when the war broke out, Hitler would bomb London with incendiaries and high explosive bombs. So when danger was approaching, at the time of the Munich crisis, we were invited to some place out in the country. But we returned immediately. There was no war – but we knew it would come. We moved with my parents into a house in Paddington. And then the second stage: when the war really broke out. Again, what to do? My parents moved from London to Bournemouth, where they lived in a little boarding-house. My mother had her piano sent there and gave lessons again. And I went to Bournemouth too. There was very little to be done. But quite soon, through Ernst Kris, I was recommended to the BBC. I went to Evesham in the Midlands, where the BBC had a listening post.[24]

What was the work?

To listen and to report foreign broadcasts. We had no tape-recorders. They did not exist at that time; instead we had wax cylinders, like the first gramophones. We recorded the speeches of Hitler and Goebbels, and other broadcasts. When they were important, we translated them in full, while other things were summarized. It was a unique experience because we saw how both sides wanted to present the war. What one called a victory the other called a defeat. I remember hearing pilots on the German radio triumphantly describing how they had dropped their bombs on London. And then when I went some time later to London, I was astonished to find the city still standing. I think now that they should have told us rather more about the purpose of our work, but that is never easy in time of war, when so many secrets have to be kept. I remember one example which was altogether typical. We always listened with particular attention to the declarations of the Vatican and the pronouncements of the Pope. But reception was very bad and as the broadcasts were repeated in several languages, all the linguists were organized so as to document the exact words and to make a composite version in English. One day I asked the head of our team, a highly intelligent man, whether the Pope had said anything important. He shook his head and said: 'No. He only talked about atoms.' Actually he was opening a physics laboratory in the Vatican and he had spoken of the power in the atom. We did not know, because nobody had told us, that it was the most important subject he could possibly have talked about. Everyone should have been avid to learn what the Pope knew about work being carried on by both sides to manufacture the atomic bomb.

It must have been rather gloomy to be always listening to news about war.

It was very hard work. It was long work, depressing. But it was a nice atmosphere. It was like being on a ship. It was a completely international crowd, and quite a large group. One of the advantages that I derived from it was getting to know many remarkable people who have remained my friends. Another advantage was that it made me more and more interested in the problem of the perception of speech and, arising from that, the problem of translation. We came across so many examples of how difficult it is to convey a German concept or phrase in English: there is often just no equivalent! Since then, this problem has never ceased to interest me. When I was awarded the Wittgenstein Prize in 1988 I made that the subject of my speech of thanks.[25]

How long did you stay in Evesham?

Only two and a half years. After that the BBC moved elsewhere. At first I was on my own, since I had to find somewhere for my wife and child to live. We were all assigned rooms in private houses in the area. There was certainly not much understanding between all these foreigners and the inhabitants of that little provincial town. They were horrified by us: first of all, these dreadful foreigners always insisted on having a bath. Of course, it cost a lot, because one had to heat the water and so on.... And they thought: 'They must be very dirty if they want to wash so often.'

After six months, I found, in a nearby village, through friends, a family that was ready to take my wife, my son and myself to live there. Surely they did not do it purely out of generosity: if they had not taken us, they might have got some slum children from London. The man was a typical country man, wealthy, rather philistine but intelligent, and through him I got to know another aspect of English life. He was always annoyed by me: I did night duty and came home at two or three in the morning. So I slept in the morning and he could not understand how people could sleep until ten in the morning. He simply could not understand it.

When the BBC moved to near Reading, we had once more to find a place to live in and it was again very difficult. That was life in the country: I had a bicycle and I rode to work. It was actually very funny because we were aliens: we had no British citizenship. And we were enemy aliens. There was a curfew: we were not allowed to leave the house, except to go to work. On the days when I was not working, I was not allowed to go out. I had a little booklet with my photograph in it, a *carte d'identité*, in which was written: 'Exempt from internment until further notice.' I was therefore not interned whereas most foreigners, including my father, were. There was a panic in 1940, when everybody thought the Germans were about to invade and all the aliens were interned and sent to camps. But they needed my work so I was exempted. And after about a year and a half, I was promoted to supervisor. I was no longer doing all the listening myself, I supervised the listening of others.

Is there any one event that made a particular impression on you during this period?

I am happy to have been the one to tell Winston Churchill and the whole world that Hitler was dead. Towards the end of the war the German radio declared that an important announcement was about to be made, and they started to play solemn music. I recognized a movement from a Bruckner symphony which he had written to commemorate the death of Richard Wagner. In order to transmit the news as quickly as possible, they asked me to listen and to write the various possibilities on bits of paper. On one I wrote 'Hitler is dead', on another 'Hitler surrenders', and so on. As soon as the announcer said: 'Our Führer has fallen in the struggle against Bolshevism,' I pointed to the corresponding piece of paper and the news was immediately telephoned to Downing Street. So I was the messenger. You might say that this is a macabre memory, but, indirectly, it was probably the most important event in which I was ever involved.

Many years later you wrote an article on this work for the BBC during the war and the meaning of propaganda, an article which is republished in your volume 'Ideals and Idols'.[26]

Yes. But I was already thinking about such matters at the time, and I wrote a long memorandum, which was never published, but which I thought I might make use of later.

An account of these years?

Not an account. It was more a reflection on the nature of propaganda.

During this period, I suppose you were completely isolated from the Warburg Institute?

No. During the war, while I was working for the BBC, I kept some contacts with the Warburg.

It did not close during the war?

No. And for a time it even stayed in London. But the librarian was killed by a bomb and the Institute moved out into a large house in the country, at Denham, where they lived rather as if on a Kibbutz. I was not entirely isolated. During the war, I gave two lectures at the Warburg Institute. I was also in contact with the *Burlington Magazine*, where I published my essay on Poussin's *Orion*.[27] And it was during the war that the publisher of the Phaidon Press, Dr Horovitz, asked whether I had something for him, because, of course, everybody was busy with the war and he had no books to publish. I had no time to write anything either but I remembered that I had started a kind of companion volume to my *History of the World* for children which was to be a history of art. Originally I had not wanted to do it, but the publisher in Vienna was keen that I should, offered more money and so on, so I did begin work. Afterwards, of course, Vienna had been taken over by the Nazis, but somebody suggested that I should try it in England. And a friend of mine started to translate the bit that I had done. So I said to Dr Horovitz: 'I have a few chapters of a history of art for young people. I don't know whether that would interest you.' And he answered: 'Give it to me, I'll show it to my daughter, who is sixteen.' Well, the daughter read it and said: 'Yes, I think you should publish this.' So he gave me a contract and he paid me an advance of £50. I started writing, but I had no time and lots of worries. Horovitz lived in Oxford, and so did my parents. When I visited them I was always afraid that I would meet him in the street and he would ask me: 'What is happening about that manuscript?' And luck was always against me. I always did meet him. In the end, I could not bear it any more. I sent him a letter saying: 'I can't do it, I return the advance.' And he said: 'I don't want your £50, I want your manuscript.' So I started again and during the war I did manage to write a few chapters of what is now *The Story of Art*. But I was really too busy with my BBC work; I had no time to write, and I put it aside and only finished it after the war.[28] All this is to show you that although I was quite seriously cut off from my real metier as a historian, I was not cut off totally.

And after the war, you came back to the Warburg?

Yes, immediately. I got less money than I had had previously, but I wanted to go back.

But meanwhile, during the war, the Warburg Institute had been taken over by the University of London. So, suddenly, I was on the staff of the University. But I had no tenure; it was renewed from year to year – not very pleasant for a man with a family.... At that time, Saxl died. He was a remarkable man, but cared little for administration. His successor, Henri Frankfort, asked me: 'What can I do for you?' I said: 'You can do something very easily, you can give me a permanent job.' And so he did. But for all those years up till then, I had no job security.

So you became an established university teacher – in the history of art, I suppose?

No! Not at the Warburg Institute. At the Warburg we taught the civilization of the Renaissance, platonism, Vasari, patronage, things of that kind. I did teach art history at the Courtauld

Institute: I gave lectures on Botticelli, Donatello or Raphael.... Naturally I also taught the history of art during the three years when I was Durning Lawrence Professor at the Slade School of Art at University College, London, not to mention the many courses I gave during my regular visits to American universities.

But by that time you had long finished 'The Story of Art'?

Actually, from the biographical point of view, the matter is very straightforward: I came back to the Warburg Institute, and resumed my work on Aby Warburg's papers, which was always a little problematic. But I had this contract to write the book on the history of art for young people. Saxl had told me not to write it but to get on with my scholarly work, and he added: 'I don't like you writing a popular book. You have other things to do.' I said, 'I'm sorry, but I have a contract.' So I arranged to have a typist come three times a week in the morning and I dictated the whole text using illustrations found in books I owned. With the help of these illustrations, I simply told the story from memory – looking at the whole subject, as it were, from a distance.

When it was finished I sent it to the Phaidon Press. For a time I had despaired of ever completing that book. I used to think that I should really write a different book altogether, which would be more an introduction to art for young people. I had actually started writing that. And when I made up the parcel to send *The Story of Art* to the Phaidon Press, it occurred to me that it had no proper beginning. So I took what I had written for the other book, and made it the introduction for this one.

I sent it. Horovitz liked it, and offered me a contract.... I have to say that writing *The Story of Art* – in so many ways a matter of pure chance – changed my whole life. Before that I was just a poor foreign scholar, who had no contacts in the great world and knew virtually nobody here. And then this book appeared and was a tremendous success. I was appointed Slade Professor of Fine Art in Oxford. One of the electors had reviewed my book, liked it and he proposed me for the professorship which Ruskin had held. This completely changed my life because, particularly in America, the prestige of Oxford is incredible – in fact, excessive! I was invited to Harvard, to Washington, everywhere.... The interesting thing is even now I lead a double life. For many people, I am the author of *The Story of Art* – they have read it at school, they had been given it by an aunt.... People know me as the author of *The Story of Art* who have never heard of me as a scholar. On the other hand, many of my colleagues have never read the book. They may have read my papers on Poussin or Leonardo, but not that. It is a curious double life.

Recently, when I gave a lecture at the Royal Academy of Arts, I don't know how many people came up to me and asked me to sign copies of *The Story of Art*. In English it is today in its 15th edition. It has been translated into nineteen languages, and it must have sold more than a million copies.

There is a curious anecdote connected with it. We decided that many of the photographs would be 'full page'. I worked on the layout with Dr Ludwig Goldscheider, a very intelligent man, who had the idea of starting every chapter on a right-hand page. But, of course, it did not always work out, because the previous chapter had to end on a left-hand page. I remember the chapter on the 12th century ended a page short. 'You must add another picture,' said Dr Goldscheider. 'I have a nice photograph at home of the Gloucester Candlestick, a fine piece of 12th-century goldsmith's work. If you write a few words about it, I can put it here.' He brought me the photograph, and I wrote something about the Gloucester Candlestick, trying to make it part of the whole story. And when the first review came out, an anonymous review in the *Times Literary Supplement*, the reviewer said: 'I was particularly interested by the remarks on the Gloucester

Candlestick.' The man who wrote this was Tom Boase, one of the electors for the Oxford chair, and an expert in 12th-century English art. And he had been impressed by what I had written!

In the years that followed you became director of the Warburg Institute.

When Henri Frankfort died, Gertrud Bing became the director for a time. Then they made me director in 1959. I used to travel a good deal, but always outside the university year. I have never taken a sabbatical, I always worked for my living. I used to go to America once or twice a year, I went to many places and got to know many American universities – all because of the reputation of that book!

What does being director of the Warburg Institute involve?

I felt it to be a great honour and a great responsibility to be in charge of an institution that included such famous scholars as Rudolf Wittkower, Frances Yates, Hugo Buchthal and Otto Kurz. Obviously, I never attempted to interfere in what they were doing. But I persuaded them to play a more active rôle in the teaching programme of the Warburg, which I reorganized.

I continued to teach, though less than before. But if you ask what the director actually does, the answer is, not very much. The real truth of the matter is that once you are in a bureaucratic machine, like the university, you have very little freedom. I discovered that very soon! The main task is to find money! I remember meetings of our committee of management when we discussed things like whether we should have our windows cleaned every six weeks instead of every four, in order to save a little money. Naturally we always organized lecture series, we invited colleagues from abroad, I had weekly meetings with our librarian to decide what books we should buy....[29]

But you succeeded in setting aside time for your own work, published a great many articles and most of your books during that time.

Yes. I think it is also true that this position gave a certain direction to my work, because I could not so easily start any long-term projects. In particular, I could not easily go to Italy and work in the archives, and that I regretted. I could not spare the time. So I gave lectures which I turned into articles or into books. *Art and Illusion* had been written before I became director. But it also started from lectures, the Mellon Lectures, in Washington. And *The Sense of Order* was another series of lectures, the Wrightsman Lectures, in New York, given when I was already director.

Do all your books except 'The Story of Art' originate from lectures?

All except *The Story of Art* and the biography of Aby Warburg. Of course the books are not simply lectures. In each case it took me years to convert the spoken word into the final text.

I had very little time. Being the director of the Warburg means being a kind of host. You have to meet scholars who come from abroad, have lunch with people, encourage students.... Scholars are lonely people. They need to be encouraged and to talk about their subjects with other people.

Do you like that kind of contact?

Yes, very much. As I often say, it is somewhat like being a broker. You hear lots of things through the academic grapevine. When somebody comes along and says: 'I am working on such-and-such,' you can say: 'I heard that so-and-so is also working on that subject. You should write to him....'

You remained the director of the Warburg until 1976, I think.

Yes, I retired in 1976. I was sixty-seven, and in those days one had to retire at sixty-seven. Now they have to retire at sixty-five. So I stopped teaching. But I didn't stop lecturing, of course.

PART TWO

There is no such thing as Art

3

THE IMPORTANCE OF TRADITION

'There really is no such thing as art. There are only artists.' This is the first sentence of 'The Story of Art.' What does it mean?

I did not invent that formulation. I found it in the writings of my teacher: in an article about 'The history of style and the history of language' Julius von Schlosser raised the question: Does art as such have a history? He was very much under the spell of Benedetto Croce, whose works he translated, and he believed that, in a way, every work of art is a spontaneous creation. Every lyrical poem exists in its own right; every painting is an 'island'. And in this connection he speaks of 'a critic arguing against the psychologist Lipps who had said that there is no such thing as art, only artists'. But this critic, added Schlosser, 'did not know that this had already been said in 1842 by someone called von Meyern.'[30] The idea behind it is of course the nominalist idea that art is a category that *we* create, and that there are different meanings attached to the word '*art*'. In the past, in the Renaissance, *arte* or 'art' meant craft, skill, technical ability. It did not mean what we mean by 'art'.

And when we today use the word 'art', what do we mean?

It has two meanings. If you talk about 'the art of children', or 'the art of the insane', you do not mean great works of art, but just paintings or images. But if you say: 'This is a work of art,' or 'Cartier-Bresson is a great artist,' you express a value judgment. These are two entirely different things which are sometimes confused, because our categories are always slightly shifting. And therefore I thought it was safer to begin by warning my reader that I would not start with a definition, because definitions are what we make them, and there is no essence of art. We can decide what we call art or not art.

It is very important in every such case to realize that all I can give is what Popper calls a 'definition from left to right', a definition in which I can say: 'In the following, I shall mean by art this or that'; what I can't say is 'This *is* art'. In the sciences, as you know, this has become absolutely accepted. Nobody asks 'what is life?' or 'what is electricity?' or 'what is energy?'. They say: 'I shall use the term energy in this or that sense.' In the humanities this Aristotelian tradition, the belief in essences, should also be abolished. It has gone on far too long. It does not get you anywhere. Every word can be given many different meanings. In that sense, I think that the category of art is one which is culturally determined. Professor Hans Belting of Munich University has written a big book[31] on the image, and insists that the idea of art only arises in the Renaissance and that medieval art should not be called art. I don't find this sort of discussion very rewarding. I have no objection to calling it art if we know what we mean. Is *haute-couture* an art? It's simply a matter of convention. There are horribly many books, which I do not read, about Marcel Duchamp, and all this business when he sent a urinal to an exhibition and people said he had 'redefined art' ... what triviality!

So that I am not sorry that I began with that sentence, although it is, of course, open to misunderstanding. The point is that there is such a thing as image-making, but to ask whether architecture is an art, or photography, or the weaving of carpets

… is just a waste of time. In German, *Kunst* comprises architecture. But in English it doesn't. If you look at the *Pelican History of Art*, you will see a volume called: *The Art and Architecture of France in the Seventeenth Century*. Every concept has a different extension in different countries.

And when you wrote your book, how did you envisage the subject?

What I actually wanted to say is that we have a right to speak of art when certain activities become ends in themselves. But it can happen with many things. In China, calligraphy is an art, which it is not in the West.

So you would propose the widest possible definition of art?

I use the word 'art' when the performance becomes as important as the function, or more important. Let me, if I may, quote a passage from the end of *The Story of Art*:

> It is the secret of the artist that he does his work so superlatively well that we all but forget to ask what his work was supposed to be, for sheer admiration of the way he did it… It was a fateful moment in the Story of Art when people's attention became so riveted on the way in which artists had developed painting or sculpting into a fine art that they forgot to give artists more definite tasks. We know that the first step in this direction was taken in Hellenistic times, another in the Renaissance. But however surprising this may sound, this step did not yet deprive painters and sculptors of that vital core of a task which alone could fire their imagination. Even when definite jobs became rarer there remained a host of problems for the artist in the solution of which he could display his mastery. Where these problems were not set by the community they were set by tradition.

But mostly, when people use the word 'art' today, they tend to mean an activity pursued for itself, unconnected with any function in society; it is a sort of mystical enterprise.

Actually, this is the result of a change that arose during the 18th century, when people began to speak of 'art' in a new sense. Until then they talked about painting or sculpture but not about 'art' as something general. That only came with the development of aesthetics and the secularization of behaviour, when contemplation became something similar to prayer. M.H. Abrams has recently written a wonderful study in which he shows that the idea that art is something elevating and holy emerged in the 18th century.[32]

This is important, from the historian's point of view. I have had to deal with it sometimes, when I was writing about Leonardo, for instance: there is all this boring stuff about how he combined art and science, but he would not have said that he combined art and science, because he did not have these notions, 'art' meant skill and 'science' knowledge.[33]

But to come back to this first sentence of 'The Story of Art': if there is no such thing as art, but only artists, did you intend to write a history of artists?

No, not really. There is a contradiction, if you like, because, just as in *Art and Illusion*, I argue that 'image making' has a history. As I said just now, the word 'art' has at least two meanings. As a result, *The Story of Art* is really two things. It is the story of how people made images, from the prehistoric caves to the Egyptians and so on, up to the present. But obviously I selected those which I also thought were works of art in the evaluative sense. So *The Story of Art* is the story of 'art' in the other sense of the word, of making good pictures.

That means that nevertheless there is something like a history...

There is a technological aspect to the history of art: one learns how to make or construct good pictures. Such pictures could not be made if one did not have the necessary technique. Perspective is an excellent example of such a technique. There are many others. In this sense, the history of art is similar to many other technical developments like, say, metal-working. It is not the same, for instance, with lyrical poetry, which has existed in one form or another in most civilizations and can hardly be said to have 'progressed'. In the history of music, on the other hand, there have been real inventions. Polyphony was an invention which changed the history of music making. The same may be true in architecture: how to make a vault over a building was not known to the Greeks. These distinctions are not unimportant.

There is a technological history, but also a history of taste, of styles, influences of one great master on another...

Yes, that is true. First of all, there is taste. But there are also the different functions of art: the purposes for which images are made are very different in different societies. In ancient Egypt many images were made for tombs, and not to be seen, except by the dead person's soul. There were no art dealers or exhibitions. From that point of view, technology interacts with many other things. I later coined the phrase 'the ecology of the image'. The image itself may evolve but its ecology, the social context, in its turn reacts back on why images are made, how they are made. Let me give you an example, a very recent one: the poster. When you make a poster, you have a definite purpose in mind: you want to attract attention quickly, so it must be simple. All these things affect, and largely condition, what the artist making the poster, say, for cigarettes, has to consider while doing it. But the same is true, up to a point, of somebody who is asked to paint an altarpiece in a church. The ecology has just as much influence as taste. Social prestige too.

Could you explain a little more fully what you mean by 'ecology'?

In biology ecology means that every species of plant or animal can only survive in a certain climate and environment. There are many circumstances which allow an organism to develop in one particular habitat, but which would prevent it developing or continuing in another. Of course, I use the word as a metaphor, but I think it is a little more precise than, let us say, the Marxist theory in which the primary production creates the superstructure that itself creates the particular style. I think there are many more factors interacting to make it likely that a particular style will prosper. And when those factors change, the art style may die out. The easiest example is the Reformation, which killed the type of art demanded by the Roman church, because the Protestants did not want images in their churches. But strangely enough, art found another ecological niche in the Netherlands. In England, it did not happen. Art was so stone-dead that they had to import artists such as Holbein or Van Dyck. Why did they have no artists of their own? Because if the young find no chance of earning a living by becoming artists, they will turn to some other profession. But in certain countries, where the tradition and the craft of painting was so strong, like in the Netherlands, they found that they could export paintings for collectors. In the early 16th century, Antwerp became a great trading centre for the export of cabinet pictures. They were exported to Portugal and to Italy. And so the workshops could continue in spite of the fact that there was no home-market for altar paintings. In England only portrait painting continued, up to a point. If collectors wanted a landscape painting, they bought it from abroad. So you find this very interesting interaction, always, between the strength of tradition and the social milieu, which allows something to continue.

Can we say that the main purpose of your 'Story of Art' was to start from the beginning of image-making and to show when and how the image became alive?

Not alive. But convincing. There is a very interesting psychological phenomenon (I have discussed it also in *Art and Illusion*): it is always the element of the unexpected that takes a work of art beyond the ordinary and shocks you into saying, 'This is alive.' If you are used to marble statues being all white and you find one which has its eyes painted, it will look unexpectedly alive. Or if you are used to pictures that do not use perspective, and you suddenly come across one where it is applied, it will look surprisingly real. Every new trick, as it were, becomes a positive – usually positive, but it may be negative – shock, until it is generally accepted and everybody takes it for granted, and then you need a new shock, like Monet's impressionism. There is a beautiful passage in Vasari. He tells how people at the end of the Quattrocento admired the paintings of Perugino, and how they thought nothing better could possibly exist, until they saw Leonardo's paintings. And then they knew there was more to be done. I think there is always this feeling of surpassing. But not in every society. There are societies which are very conservative.

The ancient Egyptian for instance.

Yes, or the Byzantines. They just wanted to have images as good as they were in the old time. It is a different attitude.

So we have to wonder why, in certain societies, an artist does want to surpass the others.

I think that there are societies where progress is at a premium and I have little doubt that this also has to do with technology and politics. In ancient Athens, it had to do with the possibility of criticism. In a country like ancient Egypt, you were probably not expected to criticize anything. But I think that once you get discussions in philosophy, for example, you get arguments – arguments in the market place about the course of politics. This is exactly what happened in Athens and in Florence. These were republics of citizens. And as soon as you have the possibility of debates, you get them in the workshop too: 'Is that the best method?', or: 'We heard that in the Netherlands they use oil for this. Is that better?' True, there are always conservatives. There is a telling remark in the *Lives of Illustrious Men* by Vespasiano da Bisticci, a Florentine author: he speaks of the beautiful library assembled by the Duke of Urbino, and he says: 'He had only manuscripts in his library and would have been ashamed of having a printed book.'

So there is a great change which originates in Greece. In 'Art and Illusion', you have a chapter called 'Reflections on the Greek Revolution'...[34]

Alluding to Edmund Burke's *Reflections on the French Revolution.* In that chapter I say that as soon as you begin trying to make a convincing, life-like image (what I called in another book the 'eye-witness' principle), you begin to introduce illusionism. Because if you really adopt the eye-witness principle, that is to say, if you want to represent a scene, as if you were standing somewhere and watching it, you have to use foreshortening, and all the techniques which lead to perspective. In the *Battle of Alexander*, in Pompeii, you could reconstruct where the observer is standing, as you can in a press photograph. With a photograph you can always ask: where was he standing when he took the picture? And this is a very important question. As soon as you adopt the 'eye-witness' principle, you have new problems but also new solutions. For instance, from where I am sitting now in front of you, I see other things in the garden than you can from where you are sitting. You can calculate what we can each see exactly because we see along straight lines. In a sense, the much discussed problem of perspective resolves itself to the fact that we see along a straight line. If something comes between me and the view out of the window, I can no longer see it.

But how do you explain – if it is possible to explain it – the birth of the 'eye-witness' principle, in ancient Greece?

I believe that it is the same, or at least parallel to, the birth of the drama. When we are watching what happens to Oedipus or to Iphigenia on the stage we witness the events of the myth as the playwright imagined them. And what was important was to shock the spectator, to move him to pity and fear, as Aristotle said. In a purely ritualistic society, you have always the same performance. Remember the Catholic ritual of the mass, with its strict rules of who stands where, and what has to be done... But in the medieval passion plays, like in Greek drama, you had a lot of realism. For instance, before the burial of Christ, you had the three women buying spices for the ointments. Usually this scene was played as comedy. There were a lot of jokes which some people might think blasphemous. But they added to the realism of the whole play. This was typical of the medieval theatre.

In the art of painting, you have something very similar. Emile Mâle, the great French art historian, in his book on the art of the 13th and 14th centuries,[35] discusses at length the techniques of meditation: a good Christian had to meditate on the stories of the Bible, such as the Crucifixion, and there were books to aid meditation, for example, that attributed to St Bonaventura, in the 13th century. He wrote: 'Imagine the scene – the Holy Virgin is sitting there – she hears something – she says 'What was that?' – it is the three Kings arriving – she is taken by surprise...'. Emile Mâle thought that this book was a very important source for art. Later critics have said that perhaps he concentrated too much on this particular text, but it doesn't matter; he was certainly right in stressing the significance of this technique used by Franciscan and Dominican preachers in the 13th and 14th centuries. Their aim was to move whole crowds of people. Friars went from town to town preaching in this way – 'Imagine what she saw.' I am sure that this movement towards a more vivid way of visualizing scenes (which must be connected with the growth of towns and the increase in population) had an enormous influence on artists.

There was a change, then, in the attitude of the Catholic Church. First the Church forgot, or suppressed, the 'Greek Revolution' towards realism in art, and then rediscovered it, because it wanted images to be more 'convincing'.

Yes, you are right. The problem was that images were forbidden by the Law of Moses: 'Thou shalt not make any graven image'. So the Church had to exercise very strict control. But little by little they realized that images could be used to teach people. I think that book by Emile Mâle is still a wonderful book.

There was another revolution in the history of art, when artists began to sign their paintings. It marks the birth of the artist as we know him. You say that this begins with Giotto.

Yes, but one cannot be too dogmatic about it. There were signatures before Giotto. In Greece for instance, artists signed vases.

But it is quite true that our idea of a great master who signs his works only began about the time of Giotto.

And at that moment art became an institution?

I think in the 14th century. It has really something to do with Giotto. People were proud of him in Florence. Cennini wrote: 'My master was a pupil of Giotto...' It becomes a line of descent.

Could we go so far as to say that this is the real beginning of art history?

Yes. I think so. You can find named artists before that, goldsmiths for instance. Nicholas of Verdun was in great demand and travelled to Hungary and to Vienna in the late 12th century. The way people wrote about art in the Middle Ages was very much modelled on the Bible and on the building of the Temple of Solomon. The idea that you can ask a famous master to come from afar is found in the Bible because Solomon asked a famous master to come from Tyre. But even so, there is a difference, a new awareness: it becomes a matter of national pride – 'Giotto is *ours!*'[36] That is what happened in Florence and it came to be traditional. And at the same time, you get the idea being formulated in the 14th century that even Giotto made mistakes. It is a way of looking at things which was to last a long time and is not over yet. So one can do better than Giotto. There was probably (I did not know it when I wrote *The Story of Art*, but I recently learned it from reading Abrams' book that I just mentioned) [37] a second change, in the 18th century, when our idea of art, first the 'fine arts', and then simply 'art', become something almost like religion, something edifying – the idea that poetry, music, painting and so on, all belong to the aesthetic sphere of art, something which one should admire and which exercises an improving influence. That was not so in the 15th century: the painter was just a painter, he was a craftsman. What happened in the 18th has to do with the *grand tour* to Italy and the transfer of certain religious attitudes to art.

There is something very striking in your book: you are always very concerned with the artist's intentions. Modern critics very often disclaim any interest in the intention of the artist.

Yes, I'm quite aware of it. And I know that they speak of the 'intentional fallacy'. Of course, one cannot always reconstruct intentions. One may be wrong, but that is true of everything. I think one must make a very important distinction between what we are sure of and what we only believe or have a hypothesis about. We can have a hypothesis about what Michelangelo wanted, though we can never be quite sure. Normally we have to rely on what Popper calls the 'logic of the situation'.[38] If you know, or if you can reconstruct, what the situation was, you can also reconstruct how a reasonable person would react to the situation. Let me give you a very simple example: if Leonardo is asked to paint the *Last Supper* in a refectory where monks are going to sit, we can assume that he will adapt the composition to reflect the way the monks are seated, and that one should see the *Last Supper* there on the wall as an extension of the room itself. There are many other cases like this where one can be pretty sure of the artist's intentions by comparing and reconstructing the situation that he faced. Someone might maintain that what he really intended to do was, say, to make fun of the monks, but that is very unlikely!

This emphasis that you give to the role of the individual leads us to another question that you stress in 'Art and Illusion'. What are styles and why do they change?

That is true. But I must confess that the book does not attempt to give the whole answer!

I suppose that is impossible.

It is impossible but one can certainly say a little more about taste than I did. What I wanted to do, there, is mainly to criticize certain assumptions, particularly in art history, that styles are a direct expression of the 'spirit of the age', a kind of super-artist who creates the things spontaneously. I remember discussions, shortly after the war, when we talked of the Gothic style, with a number of German students. They believed that Gothic cathedrals grew spontaneously out of the spirit of the age. They were surprised when I said: no, builders had to learn that style. There were pattern books, and the apprentice of one master might go to another town and build another Gothic church.... They had never thought of it in this way.

What I wanted was to go back to a more human individual level. I have always been very critical of any kind of collectivism. It is not a collective consciousness which creates a style. Somebody has to invent it. Let us say Abbot Suger of Saint Denis invented the Gothic style. Perhaps he did not, but let us say so. The question is: what made it so successful? Why did people want to copy it? Why were Gothic churches so much more attractive than Romanesque? These questions cannot be so easily answered, but some answers are possible – for instance, it appealed to a new taste, or it answered the desire to have enormous glass windows. I wrote an article not very long ago which is called 'Demand and Supply in the History of Styles':[39] first somebody wants something and then somebody else finds the means of providing it. Everywhere we have a kind of feedback, a kind of cyclical development. I like to use the example of winter sports. In the 19th century, there were no winter sports.

People did not know how to move over snow on skis. Except in Norway! But with increasing tourism, somebody in Kitzbühel bought a book about skiing from Norway around 1890 and he ordered a pair of skis from Norway and started practising. Everybody found it very enjoyable, and then there was an explosion of demand. And then everything changed. Or think of Walkmans: before they were produced by the Japanese, nobody wanted them, but as soon as they existed, everybody wanted them. These two examples, I have to say, are extreme because in these cases the supply actually created the demand.

It happens in art too that artists create a 'supply' before any demand exists. That can come about…

by a technological invention, which changes everything.

No, I was going to say, by the will to surpass other artists, which you often emphasize.

That is certainly a very important motivation in Western societies. You would not find it in India, at least in Indian art. You do not find it in this form in China. Where you do not have it, you may have very great masters – in China, for instance, there have been in every epoch artists who were recognized as geniuses in the painting of bamboo – but you don't have this chain from one to the next. In the Renaissance you certainly do have it. Leonardo said that it's a bad pupil who cannot surpass his master. And Dürer said that he saw the work of art of the future in his dreams. He would have loved to see it. There is very often this feeling that one can go on, that this is only a beginning. Cézanne saw himself as a primitive of a new age.

And we come back to the problem that we have discussed before: what does it mean to say that art has a history? What you are describing here is the way in which art becomes history.

Yes, through this feeling.

But it is not only the desire to surpass previous masters, but also to break with tradition.

Well, yes and no. If you break completely, then you will have to start quite from scratch and I don't think that is possible.

Don't you think that Impressionism was such a break?

No, Impressionism was certainly not a break. The Impressionists went on painting in a frame, on canvas. As for the problems that they set themselves, the problem of painting light, or of painting landscapes, these are problems that masters like Corot and Boudin had gone a long way towards solving.

But the Impressionists themselves thought they were breaking with tradition.

No, I don't think they thought they were making a new beginning. There is a famous letter by Renoir in which he recommends Cennini's treatise on painting. Cubism is a different matter. In the 20th century things did become different. But I believe very much that every artist must first learn the language of his art, the conventions, and only after he has mastered them, can he go on. Language is a good analogy. If you invented a completely new language, nobody would understand it.

I think the same thing holds for the philosophy of art. The only time I have written about aesthetics, about my philosophy of art, is in the chapter on I. A. Richards in *Tributes*.[40] I quote there a sonnet by him, where he says that with him it is the language which creates the poetry. And in a sense, I think that is true. Always when a great artist masters an instrument, he tries out new effects by combinations and modification. He discovers that there really are things that nobody has ever done before. In music you find that all the time. But if you start by throwing our whole harmonic system overboard, I don't think it works. I'm very critical of Schoenberg, for example. You cannot really communicate in art without a common language. The surprise effect, of which we talked before, depends on an expectation. If you expect something and it surpasses your expectation, then you are thrilled. Otherwise it is just a noise! I believe that the importance that I attach to tradition in the philosophy of art is implicit in *The Story of Art*. Perhaps I did not even know it. Later, in *The Sense of Order*, my book on decoration, I say somewhere that the shepherd boy who cut a twig from a willow tree and made a little pipe to play a tune on may have been a great genius but we cannot tell. It was only when the organ developed from that pipe and with the organ the tradition of fugue-writing could a genius like Bach arise. But you cannot go from the reed-pipe to the art of fugue in one day. Unfortunately, our modern philosophy of art does not always recognize the dependence of art on this balance between tradition and change.

Your speaking of the balance between tradition and change in the evolution of art raises a crucial question: I mean the question of progress. Can we speak of progress or is it just a series of changes which are going on? That is a difficult question.

A very difficult question. To my mind the answer is that there must always be at least a minimum of skill for us to speak of an artistic achievement. In poetry this minimum may always be assumed to be present but that is not true of the making of images. In the last chapter of the book I am writing now, on 'The Preference for the Primitive', I discuss this matter. What I say is roughly this: primitive art as we call it, tribal art, is usually very good. But Michelangelo is still better. There is progress there. But when you increase technical expertise you also increase the risks. There was bad art in the Renaissance, and there is much more now, because there are so many more ways of going wrong. It becomes more and more difficult to master this immense complexity which the medium offers. The simpler the system the fewer the risks. And therefore I think that there is both progress and regression. There is more bad art now than there was in ancient Egypt.

I am equally persuaded that the development of certain 'genres' of art (the drama with the ancient Greeks, or the novel, with Dostoyevski or Joyce) have opened up possibilities which certainly did not exist earlier.

In the latest edition of 'The Story of Art', you added a chapter on photography.

Yes. I thought: what is happening now which will be of interest to new readers? And I observed that in the last twenty years, there has been much more interest in photography as an art. And since I am very fond of Cartier-Bresson, it was a good opportunity to pay tribute to him. He wrote to me that he was '*très intimidé*'.

Do you know him?

Yes. There was going to be an exhibition of his photographs at the Edinburgh Festival and they needed a catalogue. He suggested – I did not know him then – that I should be invited to write the introduction. And I did. He liked it and he sent me a very nice letter saying that if I wanted, I could select one of his photographs as a souvenir. And he also wrote that if I wanted to visit him in Paris, I would be welcome. So I visited him, and had dinner with him one evening. And recently, we met again. He is a great master.

Why did you not add a chapter on cinema?

You are quite right to ask the question. But I do not speak in the book about moving images! I don't speak about theatre.... Actually, in my earlier years, I went fairly often to the cinema and there are films which I think are great works of art. Possibly, the greatest are Japanese: *Rashomon*, by Kurosawa, is a wonderful film. And *Derzou Ouzala.* But how would I put it into my *Story of Art*?

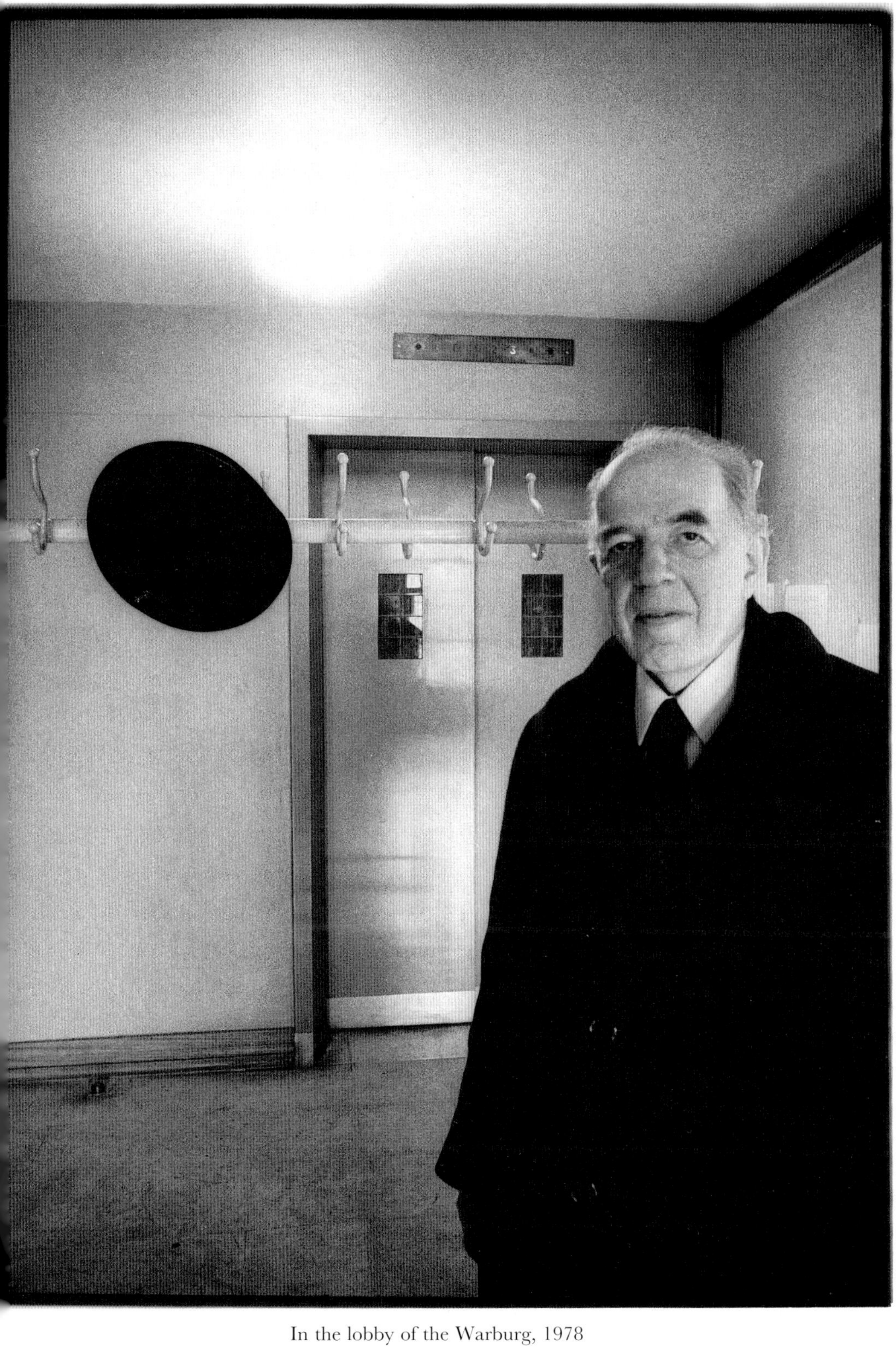

In the lobby of the Warburg, 1978

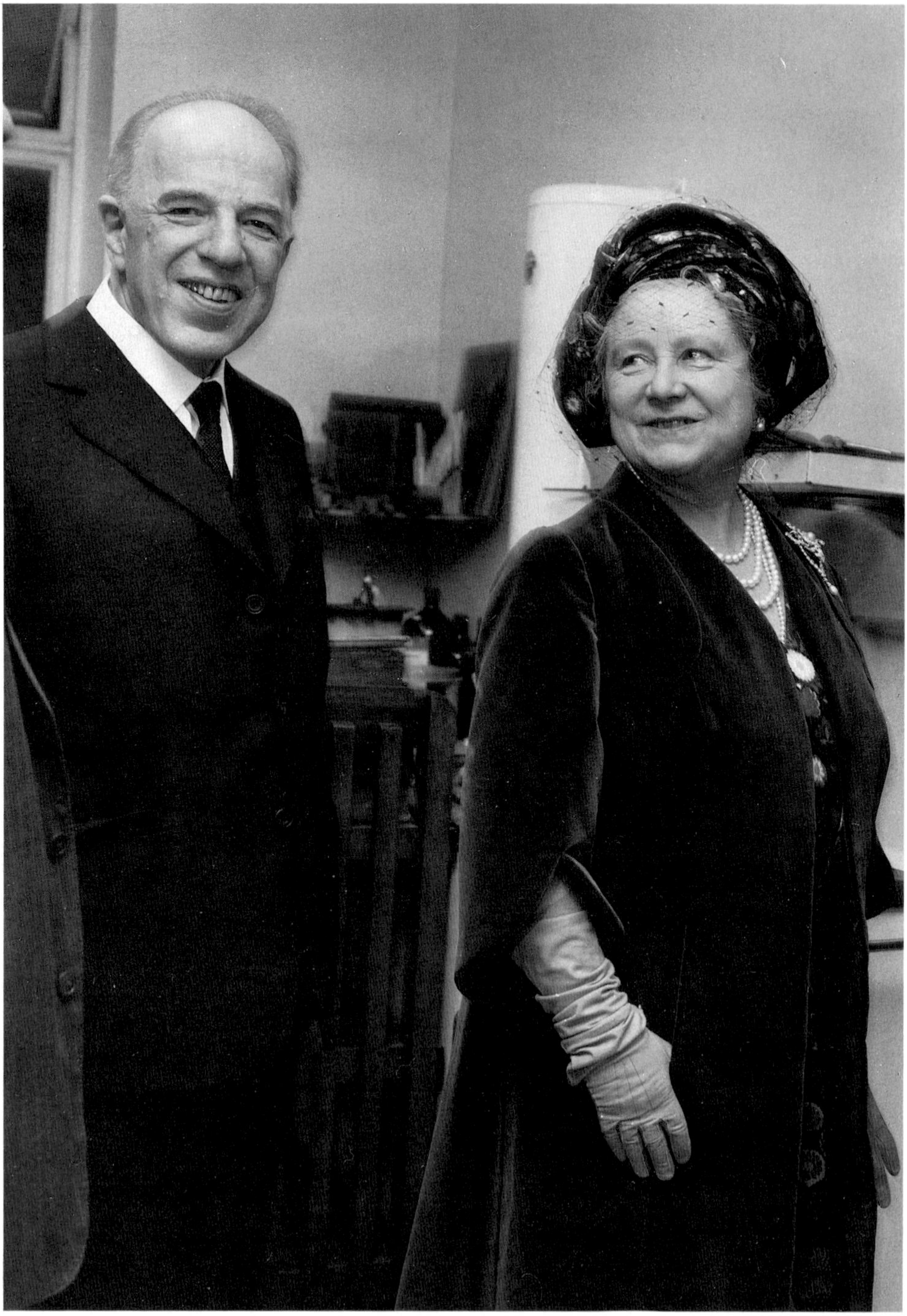

Host to the Queen Mother, Warburg Institute, March 1973

Lunch in the canteen of Cornell University while 'Professor-at-large'

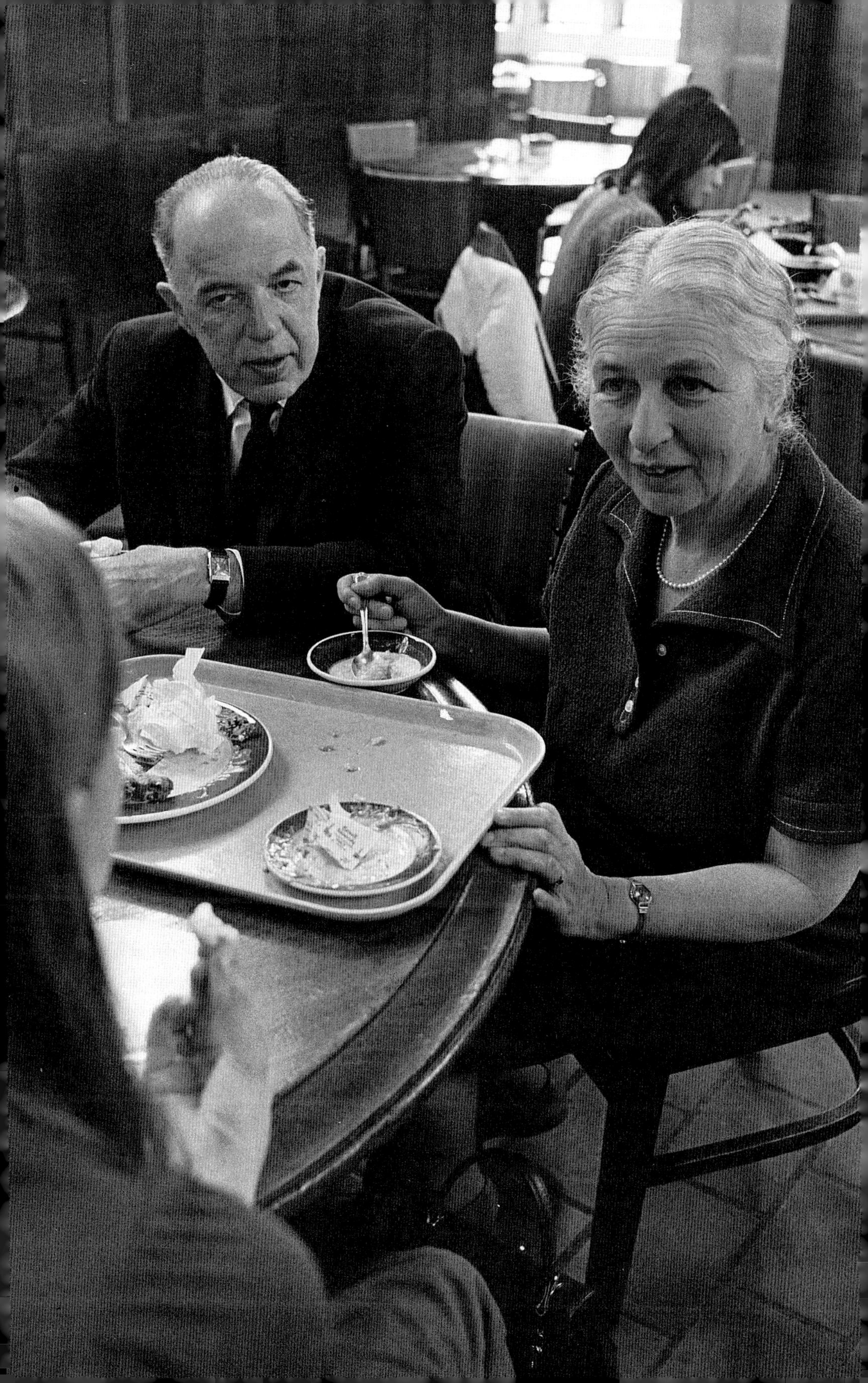

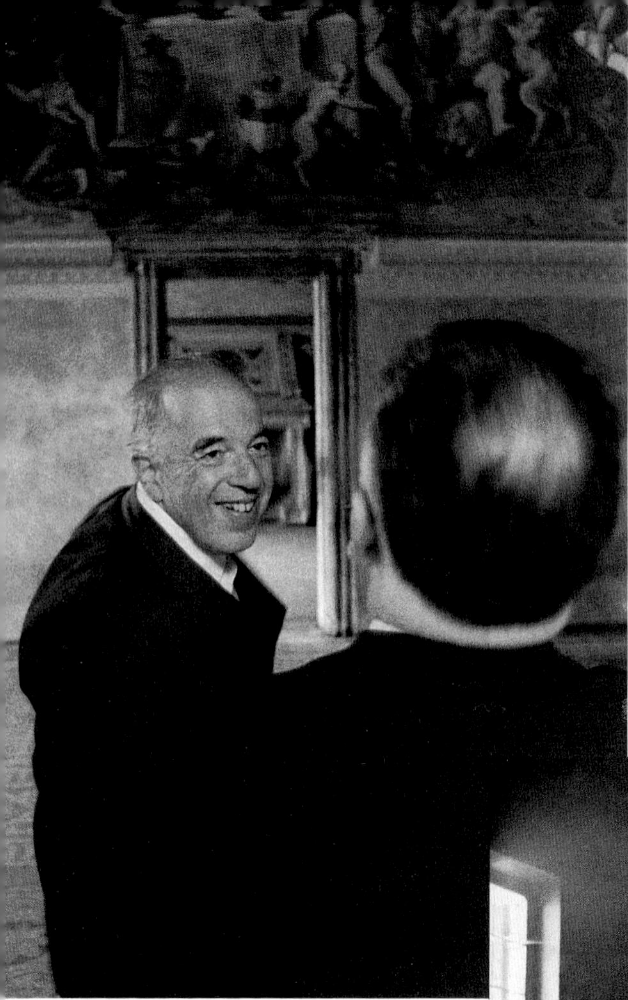

Return to the Palazzo del Tè, Mantua

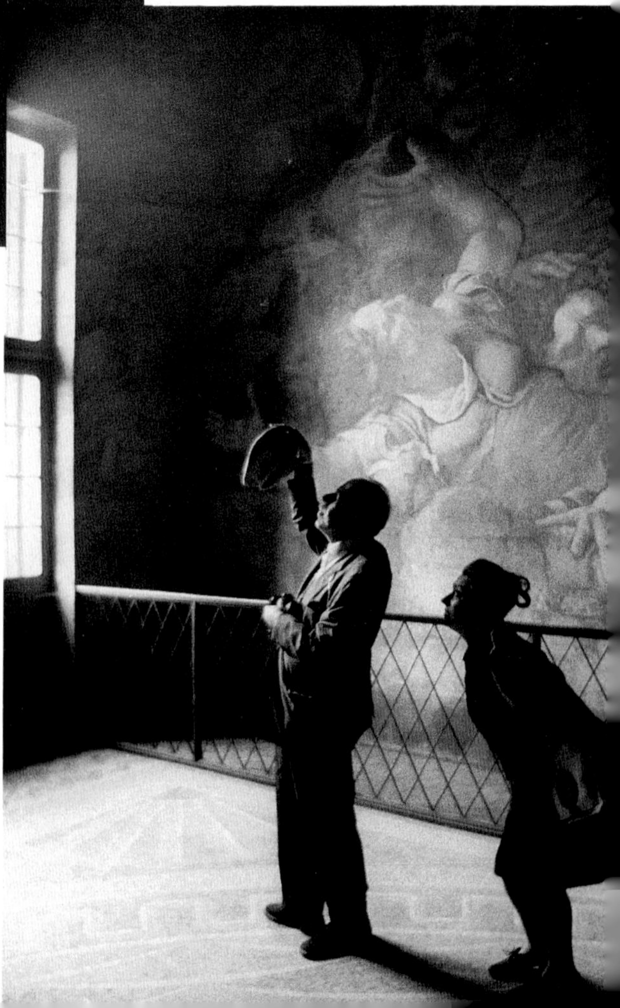

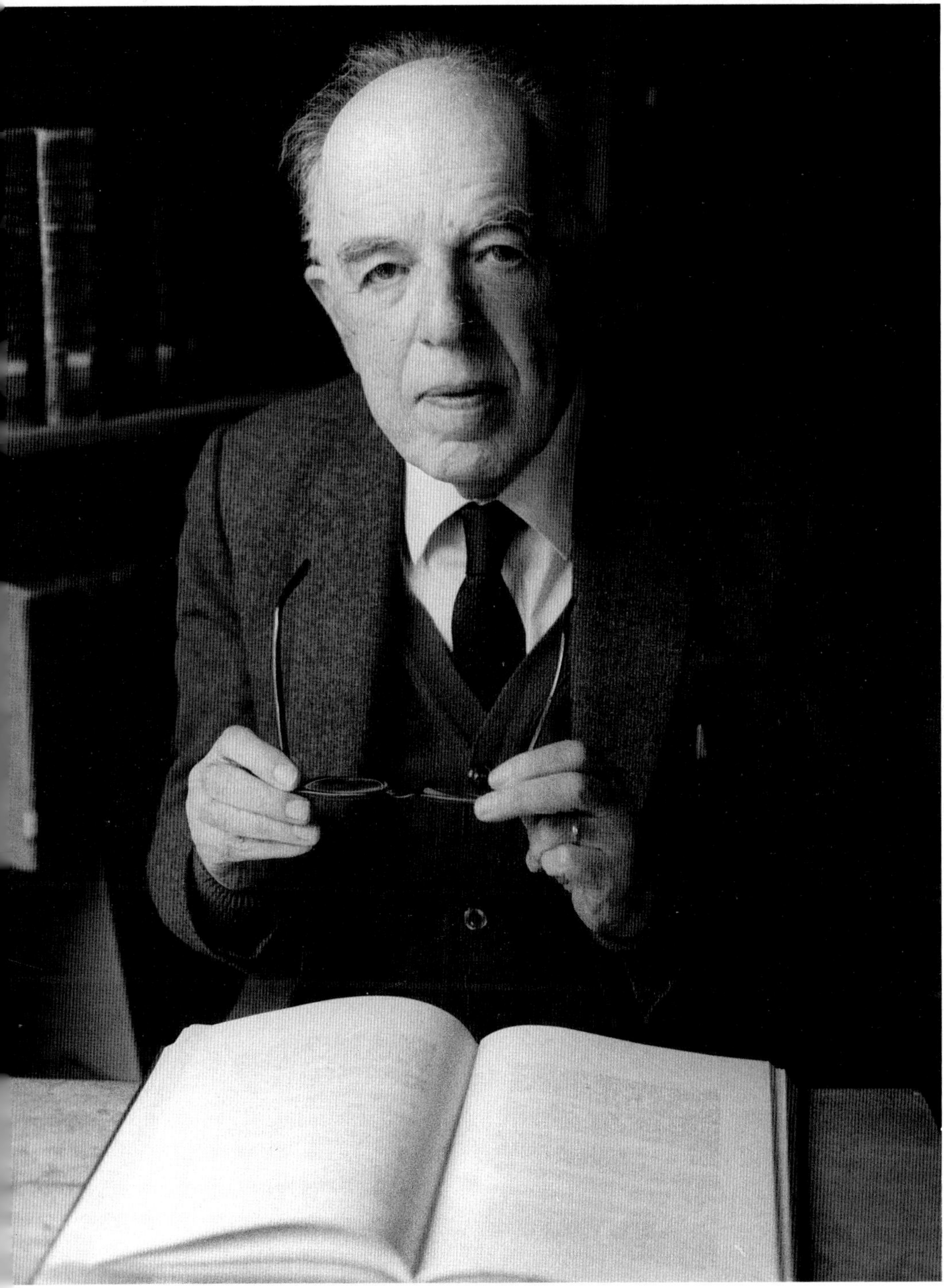

Towards the end of the Warburg directorship

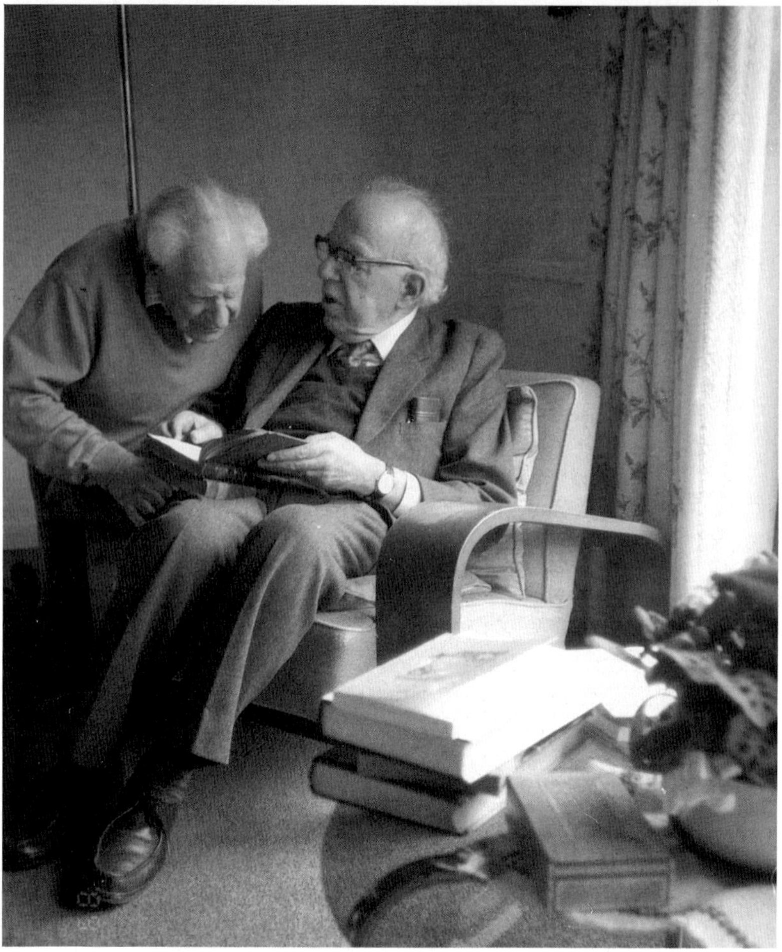

With Karl Popper
March 1989

With Didier Eribon
February 1990

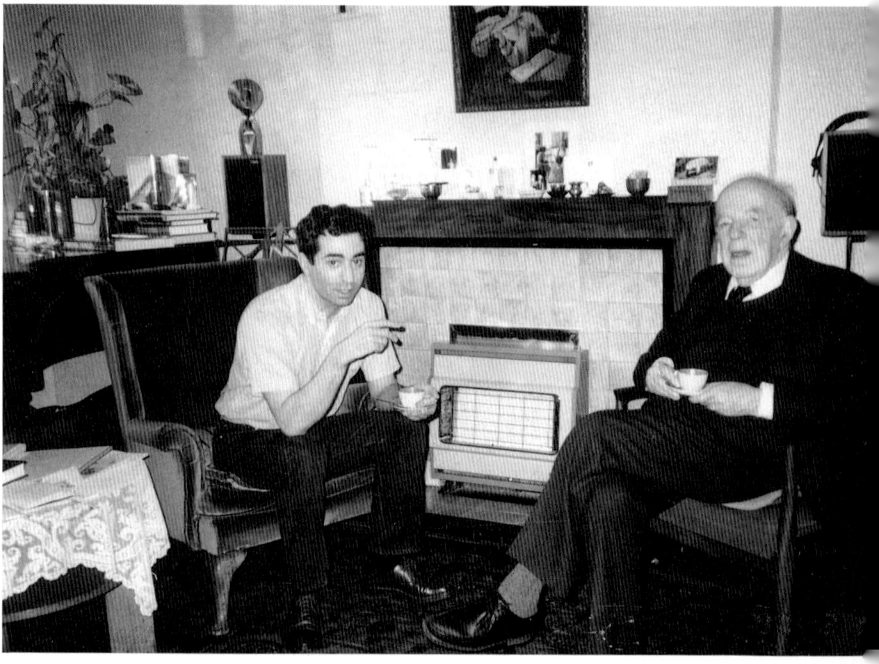

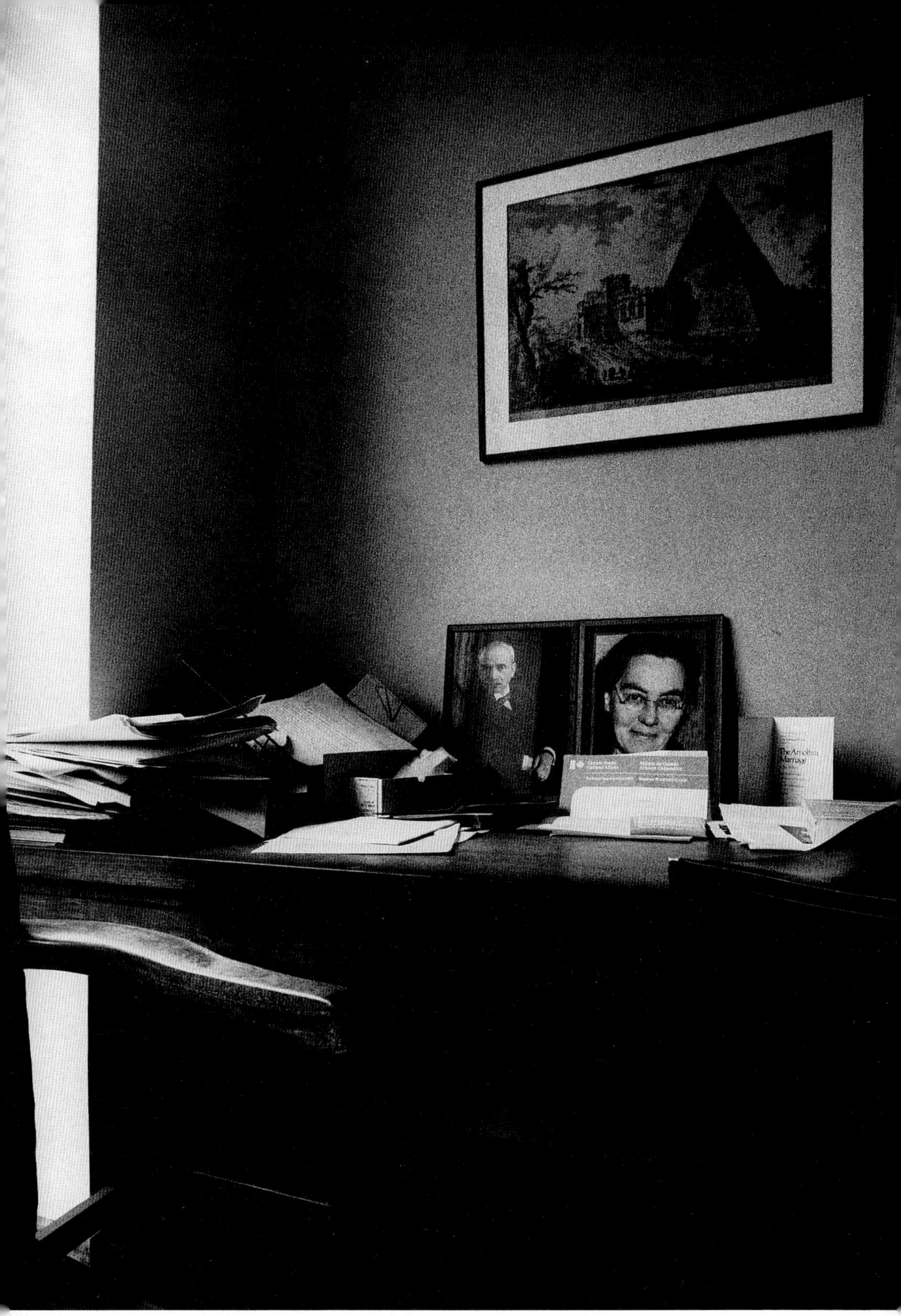

Desk at the Warburg Institute after retirement

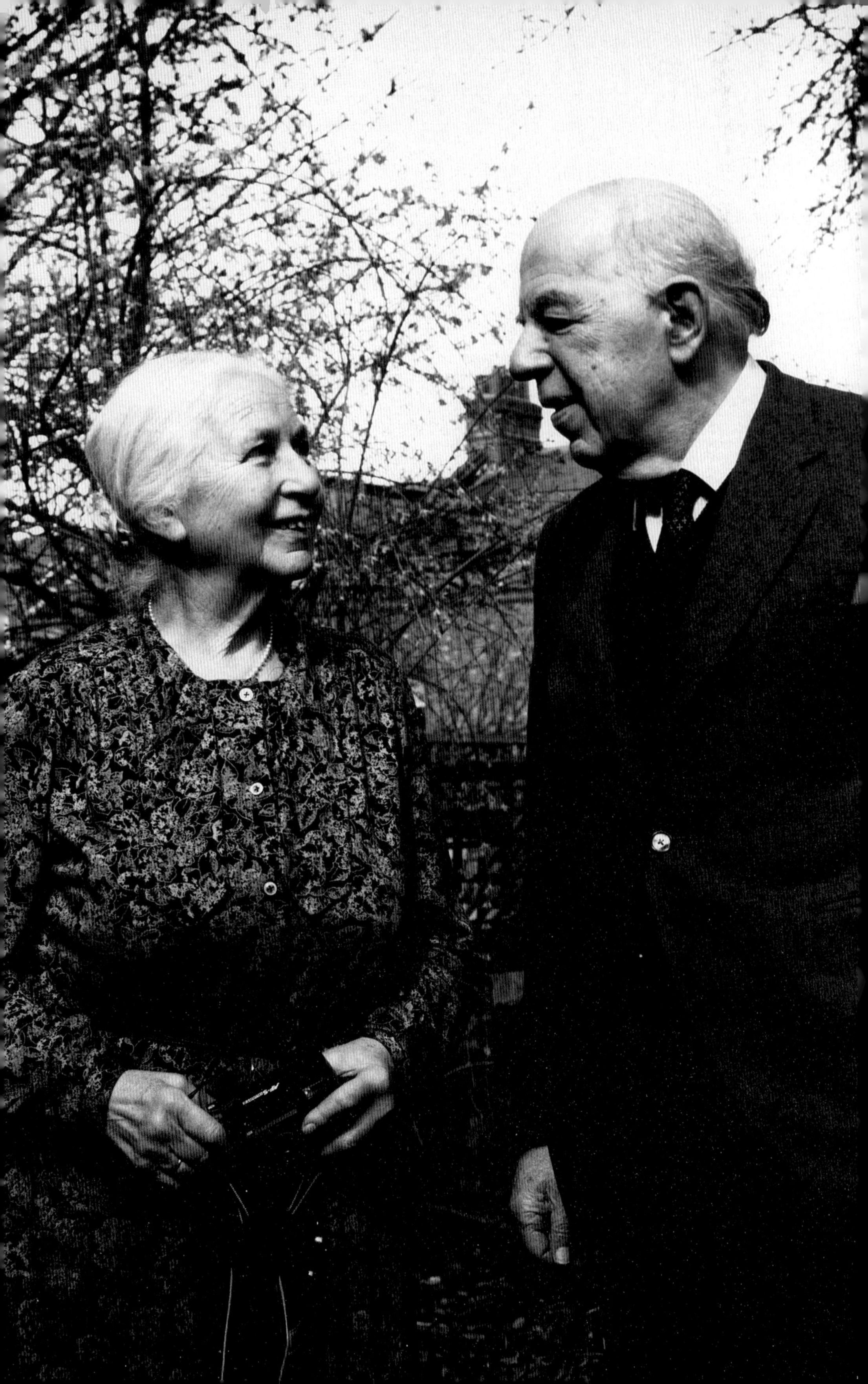

4

A THREE-DIMENSIONAL WORLD

'Art and Illusion' may be called a 'sister volume' to 'The Story of Art'.

Yes, it can be seen as a commentary on the earlier book.

At the same time it is a retelling of the story of art from another angle, and a study of 'the psychology of pictorial representation', as the subtitle puts it.

The subject of the book could be expressed in this way: What happens when somebody sits down and tries to paint what is in front of him?

How did the idea of writing the book come to you?

First of all, as I have said, I became very interested in perception during the war, when I had to listen to German broadcasts. I mentioned my interest in the perception of speech at the time. What interested me was especially the fact that in order to reconstruct and understand a blurred message you must be familiar with the subject matter. Thus hearing often depends on knowledge.[41] Naturally I wondered how far something analogous also applied to visual perception and to art.

And so, after the war and after you had written 'The Story of Art', you started to ponder the subject before tackling it directly in 'Art and Illusion'.

ement at home, Spring 1988

My starting point was certainly the traditional theory which underlies *The Story of Art*, that seeing depends on knowledge, the idea that in all representation there is an element of knowledge. In *The Story of Art* I told what was in effect the story of the progressive development of representation. And I showed how artists went from the conceptual methods of primitive peoples and the ancient Egyptians, who painted 'what they knew', to the Impressionists, who wanted to paint 'what they saw'. But at the end of the book I added that there was perhaps something contradictory in the programme of the Impressionists which led to the collapse of representation in the 20th century. Because in fact no artist can jettison all the rules and all the conventions and simply paint 'what he sees'. The way I formulated this was rather gnomic and aphoristic. In *Art and Illusion* I wanted to explain and justify what I had written, supporting my thesis this time by the findings of modern psychology.

But I have to add that I did modify my ideas in some ways. Perhaps I didn't modify them enough. Originally I thought that, really, the development went from knowing to seeing. But, partly through Popper, I realized that 'knowledge' is not quite the right word: it is more 'expectation', or 'hypothesis'. A hypothesis can be true or false. What influences an artist, when he looks at a face, is not that he *knows* that a man has two eyes, but that he *expects* – perhaps wrongly – that he has two eyes. So little by little I modified my theory: a picture is a hypothesis which we test by looking at it. And I think that what was original in my book was not that I was asking how we see the world but how we see pictures. I learned from the great American psychologist James J. Gibson that we never see the world as a flat picture.[42] But, strangely enough, we do see a flat picture as if it were the world. As I sit here, I do not see a flat thing: I see you, sitting on your chair, and everything around you. So the miracle worked by painting, I mean naturalistic painting, is precisely this reduction onto a flat surface of that which cannot be reduced to two dimensions. That we can do that is an impossible paradox. The real problem of naturalistic art, when all is said and done, is just this paradox.

And this explains why so many art styles never make the attempt at all: ancient Egypt is a famous example, but you find the same thing in tribal art. In Africa and in Mexico, and everywhere else you find the same approach: you construct an image, which in my book I call a 'minimum model'. Think of children's toys, the simplified model of a train or a car, which are very analogous to the simplified model of a man in tribal sculpture. The idea that the artist should be the 'eye-witness' does not occur. And my point, later on, had often been that we are looking at it from the wrong point of view when we call all these styles 'primitive'. They are not. When they adopt the method of 'conceptual representation', and create images in a pictographic way, they are doing the natural thing. It is we, when we try to create naturalistic images, who are doing the unnatural thing. So I prefer to call what we used to call 'primitive art', 'two-dimensional coding'.

One could say that your book is sustained by this wish to understand the paradox of naturalistic painting – how it can imprint on a flat surface something that we see as a three-dimensional world – and to elucidate by analysing the act of perception what this 'illusion' is which figurative art produces.

It is easy to show that, when we look at a naturalistic painting, we have to interpret the two-dimensional forms in terms of objects in space. We understand this, and we see an image for what it essentially is: the projection of a three-dimensional form on a flat surface. Yet the process of interpretation easily goes beyond the elements on the canvas. We have a tendency to add what we assume to be there. Numerous psychological experiments have shown that these projections can never be completely suppressed or separated from the basic visual sense data.[43]

In my writings I have stressed that these phantom images are not just curiosities: they tell us a great deal about the role of the imagination in perception. It may never be possible to separate exactly what we really see at any one moment from what we remember or expect. The expectation or anticipation can produce the illusion or phantom of a perception. I make the point in *Art and Illusion* that conjurers often exploit this tendency of our minds, but in the chapter on 'Illusion and Art' in the book that I published with Richard Gregory I went even further and speculated that even animals may be subject to this kind of illusion.[44] I took the example of a dog who wants his master to throw a stick so that he can bring it back. I suggested that the dog no less than we can be deceived by the master *pretending* to throw the stick, but actually holding on to it. For a brief instant, we imagine that we see the stick flying through the air, and the dog will also run after this phantom. I wrote at the time that I did not think this hypothesis could ever be verified. But to my surprise and pleasure I received an offprint last year from a neurobiologist who believed that he could show that monkeys in his laboratory had these phantom visual anticipations.[45] Now, if his observation is at all correct, it follows that such anticipatory phantoms are not the exception but the norm. In other words, if the stick really had been thrown, we (or the dog) would have also seen, for a split second, a phantom stick leaving the master's hand, but this illusion would fuse and be modified by the sight of the real stick, and would become irrelevant. It is relevant only in the exceptional cases of arrested movement and arrested vision.

Since my starting-point in *Art and Illusion* was, as I said, the perception of pictures and not the perception of reality, it was inevitable that I concentrated on those effects of our imagination which tend to transform what we actually see. It is understandable that these observations interested readers of the book particularly and they formed the wrong impression that I regarded perception as an entirely subjective matter. Perhaps I should have warned them more explicitly against this misunderstanding, but I was happy to find that a careful reading of my text would have saved anyone from this mistaken interpretation, particularly in the section where I refer to the theories of J. J. Gibson.

Could you expand on this rather crucial point?

The matter is somewhat technical but I'd like to explain it as simply as possible. Basically it concerns the role which *guessing* plays in our perception. Gibson knew perfectly well that there are situations in which we have to rely on guessing. There is a beautiful chapter in his book on *The Senses Considered as Perceptual Systems* in which he discusses perception in reduced visibility such as fog or dusk when, as he said, 'the system begins to hunt', trying out and testing a variety of hypotheses about what is out there in front of us. But his real contribution to the theory of visual perception lay precisely in the discovery that the role of guessing in our response to the visual world has been much exaggerated in traditional psychology because our perception – and that of animals – is geared to *movement.* When we walk towards an object in our environment such as a table, the image on our retinas will be constantly transformed and he could show mathematically that these transformations reveal to us precisely the underlying invariant shape of the table. He admits that in what he called 'snapshot vision' the rectangular table-top will appear as a trapezoid, but we do not have to *guess* that the trapezoid represents the projection of a table, we will *see* this as soon as we move.

Now, as we have seen, it is precisely in 'snapshot vision' that guessing plays a vital role. After all, you might say that if you see a flat picture you can only *guess* that it represents a three-dimensional reality, or, to put it in other words, you have to imagine the reality behind the flat picture. This may sound unnecessarily pedantic. Who wants to be told that the Mona Lisa is a flat panel covered with pigment and that we are only made to imagine the woman behind it? But there are well-known tricks which remind us that here our guesses can be manipulated and can be wrong. One of them is the trick of anamorphosis, which may have been invented by Leonardo himself, and which plays with the perspectival projection of objects on an oblique surface at which we are made to look through a peephole. Viewing the picture like that, we believe we see a normal portrait, but what is *really* behind the peephole is a grotesque distortion. There are more sophisticated forms of this game developed in the psychological laboratory of Adelbert Ames which I also mention in *Art and Illusion*.

Gibson was not much interested in this kind of trick, because it seemed to him much too artificial and to tell us nothing of the way we really see the world. Since even if we may make false guesses when looking at the world, these, as I indicated, are immediately refuted by the stream of information which results from movement. This is what I wrote and still believe to be true: 'Our belief that we can ever make the world dissolve into such a flat patchwork of colours rests in itself on an illusion, connected, maybe, with the same urge for simplicity that makes us see the indeterminate sky as the vault of heaven. It is to the three-dimensional world that our organism is attuned, where it learns to test its anticipations against the flow of incoming stimuli, weeding out or confirming the predictable melodies of transformation that result from movement.'[46] I think today that this passage should have been developed and that I should have insisted rather more on this point. This is why I was afterwards not so surprised that my theory of perception was somewhat misunderstood. Perhaps it is not easy to understand. But I believe that it implies truly a very important change of attitude.

Was your interest in psychology in line with the work you had done with Ernst Kris in Vienna?

Yes, the direction that my work took was certainly determined by my collaboration with Ernst Kris. But I should add that it was equally influenced in a more general way by my having grown up in Vienna. Because interest in psychology was endemic in the Viennese school of art history at that time, ever since Aloïs Riegl, about 1900, wrote his book on the applied arts in late Antiquity.[47] In this work, and in his other writings, he postulated that art passed from a stage that he called 'haptic', that is, relying on touch (in ancient Egypt, for example, where objects are rendered in art such as they are revealed by the sense of touch), to an 'optic' phase, when art relies solely on vision, as was the case in late Roman Antiquity, with an intermediate stage of Greek Antiquity. I did not believe it very much, but it certainly gave my researches a purpose: to analyse the role of perception in art. So Riegl was one source. But there was the rival idea, I also derived from Vienna, and mainly from one of my teachers, a very old man, a retired archaeologist, a friend of Freud, called Emanuel Loewy. My book is dedicated to his memory. Loewy, around about the same time as Riegl, wrote a fundamental book on the imitation of nature in Greek art, in which he studied the transition from archaic art to classical art and later.[48] And it was he, mainly, who stressed the schematic character of early art and the gradual modification of the schema: at first, bodies are very rigid, and then they start to move… In other words, Greek art, as he saw it, never directly imitated visual appearance, but it was the other way round: it gradually approximated to it.

It was really this idea which was applied to medieval art by my teacher Julius von Schlosser, who was interested in what at that time was called 'the conceptual image (*Gedankenbild*)', which resembles the way children draw: the child does not imitate, but creates symbols, schemata which gradually approximate to visual appearances. Schlosser wrote a very good book on medieval art, in which he stresses this.[49]

So, this idea that when he makes a representation an artist does not start by simply looking, but by thinking, is certainly not mine. It is an old idea. Only I was perhaps a little more radical.

In many of these accounts, there was a certain contrast between, on the one hand, the way in which a child, a primitive or an ancient Egyptian constructs an image, purely intellectually, and, on the other, a realistic painting by a Dutch painter of the 17th century. My idea was that it is more a difference of degree, a spectrum, and that one never gets to the very end, not even the Impressionists, who believed that they were getting rid of what they only *knew* and relying exclusively on what they *saw*.

So the thesis of my book is that there is no 'innocent eye'. The term 'innocent eye' comes from Ruskin. In a very good little book, called *The Elements of Drawing*,[50] Ruskin said that if you want to draw, you must forget what you know and only look. And I say: you cannot forget what you know.

I can well understand that your Viennese background gave you this interest in psychology, but after you went back to the Warburg you could have confined yourself to research in art history proper, or rather, let us say, more generally, the history of civilization.

After the war, when I rejoined the Warburg Institute, everybody was interested in Neoplatonic symbolism, and I did historical research on Botticelli and subjects of that sort. I published a number of articles. But I wanted also to write a more ambitious work of which actually *Art and Illusion* and *The Sense of Order* are only fragments: a general book on images and the different functions of images. It was to include illustration, symbolism, emblems and decoration. I have somewhere a long project which I submitted to a publisher and which I called *The Realm and Range of the Image.* Then I was invited to give the Mellon Lectures in Washington. It was Kenneth Clark who suggested they should invite me because he liked an article I had written. So I had to think of a subject. As I told you I had been Slade Professor in Oxford, and one of my series of lectures was about the various techniques of drawing. I called one lecture 'The Conjuring Brush', and I traced how painters had gradually relied more and more on the spectator: 'conjuring brush' meaning the painter working like a conjurer, like a magician. So I had the materials for this, and I put the series together. For instance, I had talked in Oxford about Constable's drawings. So I thought: with this general framework, I should be able to make seven lectures for Washington.

I called the series 'The Visible World and the Language of Art'. So it was a kind of linguistics of the image. I think it was a good title, but the publisher did not want it because it was too long. He wanted something shorter, but still with the word 'art' in the title. So I made a long list of combinations, 'Art and Nature', 'Art and Vision', etc. And I consulted my friend Popper who selected 'Art and Illusion'. So that was the title that we chose. I have often regretted it since, because people always think that I only appreciate paintings which create illusions. But that is how life goes. People don't even read the subtitle! Which is 'A Study in the Psychology of Pictorial Representation'.

Your book deals with the advances, technical and otherwise, that led to the achievement of realistic representation, the production of real illusion. You describe this process in terms of trial and error, an approach which you derive from Karl Popper. First one creates an image, then one sees whether it resembles the object, and finally one corrects what does not correspond.

Yes, it is a matter of constructing a hypothesis and testing it. And this testing is precisely what an artist does when he steps back from the canvas and looks at what he has painted.

In your lecture at the Pompidou Centre in 1987,[51] *you quoted the reply of Whistler to one of his pupils.*

Yes, when the pupil said: 'I paint what I see,' Whistler answered: 'Indeed, but just wait and see what you have painted.'

That little exchange would be a good way of summarizing the problem you are talking about in 'Art and Illusion'.

Yes. We may say so.

The history of Western painting consists of trial and error, of 'making and matching'?

Yes: 'schema and correction'. A number of critics misunderstood this, and thought that because I say that we can never imitate what we see, I also say that everything is relative, that is to say that Egyptian art is just as correct as a modern realistic painting. This I do not believe. The two images affect us very differently. Think of an expressive face or an erotic nude. The more it becomes like the real thing the greater the psychological effect. And how was that resemblance achieved? You had to learn! And it took a long time to learn. It took three generations at least and probably more in ancient Greece and again in the Renaissance.

More than three generations between the Byzantine manner and Michelangelo. Many more than three generations. So you get this method modifying the hypothesis till it fits. And of course, even then, people were very much more aware of the fact that further innovations were still possible. In the Renaissance you could not paint a still life like a Dutch 17th-century painter or like Chardin. Not everything is possible in every age.

So what we have to do is to study the schemata that were available to artists in each period?

Yes, to find out what the repertory of the period was.

In your book you distinguish three important steps in the history of representation: the first is ancient Greece, the second the invention of perspective, and the third, before the Impressionists, is Constable.

You are absolutely right. We talked about the Greek Revolution, the 'eye-witness principle' and the parallelism with drama, with Greek tragedy. The return of this principle in the Renaissance is less described in *Art and Illusion* but it is discussed elsewhere in my writings. Finally, in the 18th century, we encounter the increasing awareness more and more, that however much we try to be realistic, we have still, as they said, a manner, '*manière*'. Constable was obsessed with it: one must get rid of manner, he thought.

He wanted to be like a scientist, or what he thought a scientist was: just discovering the laws of nature.

Yes. It is again the idea of the 'innocent eye'. Naturally, if one could represent a tree without any 'manner', one would be like a photographic camera, and nobody could tell who had drawn it.

Art history depends on the fact that we can recognize the 'manner' of Renoir and of Manet. Otherwise it would all look exactly the same!

As you rightly say, Constable believed that he could be like a scientist and paint without prejudice. Without preconceptions. And then I also discussed, up to a point, the breakdown of this claim. One of the reasons for this breakdown, where *Art and Illusion* stops, is photography. But also the fact that painting had actually achieved complete fidelity to appearances, perfect *mimesis*. There were of course other reasons, connected to this one. But it is an important reason: the change in the attitude of what can be done, and of course the rivalry with photography, when the artist is wanting to do something different, something photography cannot do.

To come back to Constable, do you consider him as a very important artist?

Well, I admire him as a very original and lovable painter, but what made him so important for me was that he reflected so much about his work: we have his letters, his lectures; he was very self-conscious. This was very welcome to me for my project. I don't think you would find a single line which Chardin wrote about his art. Otherwise I might have taken Chardin as an example. There are other artists who were self-conscious. Delacroix was. But very few were as revealing as Constable, for this particular phase in the history of art. For another phase Leonardo, of course, was still more important.

Impressionism marks a turning point in the theory of 'the innocent eye'.

Yes, because it was the moment when artists thought they had arrived at seeing nature as it is.

So they imagined that they had arrived at the final point. And in a sense it was the final point. For figurative painting, at least.

Yes. You know, Cézanne is very important here. He was probably more of an Impressionist than people usually say. He was after all a pupil and an admirer of Pissarro. But the Impressionist formula did not satisfy him. He always aimed at something which he called 'les petites sensations'. And this is of course something much more subjective. He often despaired and discarded what he had begun and started again. In this struggle to '*réaliser*', he called it, he was even prepared to get rid of perspective, because he did not see the world in perspective; what we see is modified by what psychologists call the perceptual constants. As Voltaire said, when I see a friend going away, if the distance doubles, he does not diminish by half.[52] In Cézanne, you get these enormous tensions. He is such a great master because he did not try to camouflage these problems. It is his astonishing struggle to do something which cannot be done that makes him such a great artist.

Do you like Impressionist painting?

Very much, particularly Pissarro. I also like the best Renoir. Monet, of course. But Monet is uneven. Sometimes he is a little facile. Sometimes he is a little too formulaic. But the serial paintings we saw at the Royal Academy in 1990 show again how very hard he worked at his problems.[53] These are all explorations of the pictorial effects of light. He wanted to recreate for instance how the waves on the river Thames reflect the light. He couldn't paint them in the open air *sur le motif.* He painted them in his studio. I am pretty sure that he took photographs and then studied how to use them as a *schema*. But I told you that I am particularly fond of Pissarro. If you ask me what the world looks like to me, it looks like a painting by Pissarro.

Do you think we can see the world as a picture? Can pictures teach us to see?

Up to a point they can. When you spend an hour or two in a museum, and then go out, suddenly, the world is transformed. Particularly, we see human faces differently. We see the shadows, the colours.... We see the world a little like a painter.

In your book called 'The Image and the Eye',[54] *which is in some ways a continuation of 'Art and Illusion', you are not so affirmative.*

Because Gibson convinced me that eyes were given to the animal species so that they may orientate themselves in the real world. Normally they serve that purpose admirably. When I see the traffic jams in London I am always astonished that there are not more accidents. The reason must be that even the least skillful motorists can sum up their own situation and that of the other cars both in front and behind. And, just as people all over the world learn to drive very quickly and to extricate themselves from traffic jams, I am sure that people of all periods have acquired the skill of using their eyes to orientate themselves in various situations. What we learn is attention, the ability to concentrate on certain things. But one can develop this ability in all sorts of different ways. For example, if you are a meteorologist you will see clouds differently. I am sure that the pilot of an aeroplane does not see clouds as you or I see them. I have no doubt that perception can be trained to see very different aspects of the world. And as a result, looking at pictures does teach us how to direct our attention.

But one should not carry this line of thought too far. I do not think that it is correct to say that people in the 12th century saw the world differently. They did not, but since there is no innocent eye, we are also influenced by our knowledge. I am not so sure that we can see the moon as we saw it thirty years ago. We are influenced by our memory of what we saw on the TV screen and our knowledge that the surface of the moon is black, like charcoal. Some people have been much too extreme in talking about the modification of perception through art. One of them was Kahnweiler. He really did believe that the artist creates the world for us.[55] So one day we shall all see the world in a Cubist way.

But in a sense we do see the world in a Cubist way.

Up to a point. Have you seen the photographs by David Hockney? They are composite photographs, a sort of mosaic which juxtaposes different points of view. In the fifteenth edition of *The Story of Art* I reproduced one of these Hockney photographs. We learn to pay attention to the composite aspect of vision, and this creates the effect of mosaic.

What was Gibson's reaction when he read your book? You are a Gibsonian, but was he a Gombrichian?

Not at first! He wrote a very critical review of my book. Later I became 'Professor at large' at Cornell University where I went once in a while, and we had many talks. He was changing his mind all the time about pictures. He knew a great deal about our perception of the world, but he did not really know so much about pictures. He was very uncertain. He did not believe in illusions created by art because he did not think that the perception of reality can be mediated by a picture. But in the course of a discussion with him, in the journal *Leonardo*,[56] I said: 'It is true that I see the chair in the round and not only one aspect, but what about Mont Cervin? I don't see the whole mountain when I am in Zermatt.'[57] When I saw him at Cornell, he said: 'About Mont Cervin, you are of course right.' And I was a little disappointed that he never admitted this in public. That is not entirely true, however. He did write about it to a correspondent who later showed me the letter.[58] He was, as I said, always uncertain about what a picture really is.

After the publication of 'Art and Illusion', there were a lot of discussions, and some people read it as a defence of representational painting. This is a very strange misunderstanding.

The book is intended as an investigation, not as advocacy. It is nonsense to think that I only like naturalistic art. First of all, I like music, which is not a realistic art. I like architecture. I like decoration.

But in painting as such?

Well, I should say that I have a certain response to the mastery of the métier, to masters such as Velazquez or Chardin. I saw the Chardin exhibition in Paris and it was miraculous.[59]

Among your readers was the American philosopher Nelson Goodman, who discussed your book in his well-known book, 'Languages of Art'.[60] *You seem very reluctant to comment on the interpretation he gave.*

He rather misunderstood my book. He interpreted it as completely 'conventionalist'. He wanted to assimilate artistic images to language. The word 'horse' has no resemblance to an actual horse. The meaning we give it is purely conventional. Goodman and those who follow him wish to convince us that similarly the image of a horse has no resemblance to an actual horse, and that we recognize it as a horse only because we have learned the convention. It is a strange doctrine, since even animals sometimes recognize images. I know Nelson Goodman very well. I wrote an article in the volume of essays in his honour.[61] We get on very well as long as we don't talk about these matters. You know, he was an art dealer originally. He is very interested in art. And when he is here, in London, he always tells us about the pictures he has bought.

But I feel very proud, because in *The Image and the Eye* I quote a letter that he wrote me where he more or less retracts: 'I do not hold the extreme views which are often attributed to me',[62] he says. But, anyway, I think his views are indeed extreme. He denies that anything can be like anything else. A picture cannot resemble reality. In the terms used by the medieval scholastics he is a strict nominalist. He wrote an article, not long ago, in a symposium in which I also took part, in which he denies that we can speak of pictures in the mind.[63] But anybody who ever had a dream has experienced such pictures, whatever we may want to call them.

In the first pages of 'Art and Illusion', you mention three men who are the main inspiring sources of that work: Köhler, Kokoschka and Jakobson. Isn't it a strange trilogy?

Yes, it is. I met Wolfgang Köhler, the great Gestalt psychologist, in Princeton. He was a very impressive man. I paid tribute to him in another article.[64] The first thing I did when I met him in a classroom in Princeton was to draw a little face on the blackboard, like the faces children draw, a round shape with two dots for eyes, a stroke for a nose and another for a mouth. And I said: 'I want to find out what is going on when we recognize a face in this drawing.' And he said: 'Much too complicated. Psychology is still a baby, we have not yet reached that stage.'

The afternoon that I spent with him was a very interesting and very moving experience. He had a great disappointment in pursuing his theory: he hoped that he would prove what he called 'isomorphism', that is to say that the events in the brain correspond to things outside. And he wanted to prove it by making a cat look at a certain shape, and recording the so-called 'alpharhythms'. It never worked. Because it is just not possible. My friend Richard Gregory, another psychologist, says something malicious but correct: he says that the *Gestalt* people believe that when you see a circle there is a circle in your brain. And when you look at green, is there green in your brain? That is really why I am not a *Gestalt* psychologist.

In *Art and Illusion* I pay homage to Köhler because he always insisted that a researcher should never restrict the area of his inquiry. I have found that more than an encouragement.

And Jakobson? Did you know him?

Indeed yes. He has even been here, in this house! I met him when I taught at Harvard summer school. And we also came together for one weekend at Cape Cod, a seaside resort not far from Cambridge, Massachusetts. I have had quite a number of talks with Roman Jakobson, and I learned a lot from him. I learned something fresh from him about language. He was an amazing person. He was very tall, very strong and very ugly. He was also very fascinating. One day we were talking about synaesthesia and he mentioned that Mallarmé has said that *jour* ought really to mean 'night' because of the sound of the words. I mentioned this in *Art and Illusion* and I have remained fascinated by the role of synaesthesia in language and in metaphor.

We could add a lot more names to those that you refer to and quote.

Yes, and particularly, at that time, it was the psychologist Jerome Bruner. I knew him very well. He also played quite a part in my ideas and in my life. I saw him in Harvard and we were a good deal together and I served as a subject for experiments in his laboratory.

The least we can say is that your American journeys were very profitable intellectually speaking!

Yes! I also met Ulric Neisser. He was very important for me too. He was a student and successor of Gibson at Cornell. He rang me not very long ago and asked whether I would accept an honorary degree in Atlanta, where he is now. So I went there in May 1991. I much enjoyed talking to him. I think his book on cognitive psychology is the best I know.[65] He tries to make a kind of synthesis between what Gibson said and more traditional views. He wrote a lovely book called *Memory Observed*, an anthology of how people remember and a discussion of the various forms of memory. Now he is writing a book on the self, on the development of the ego in children.

And I have already mentioned Richard Gregory, with whom I worked on an exhibition on 'illusion', which became a book.[66]

So, if I may say so, you have two lives as a scholar: a life as an art historian and a life as a student of psychology.

Well, I have never claimed that I am an expert in psychology.

But you read a lot in that field.

Before I went to Washington to give the Mellon Lectures I spent a good deal of time, over a year or two, in the library of the

British Society of Psychology. I wanted to know what contemporary psychologists were saying about the theory of visual perception.

And now?

Psychologists were interested in my book, so they send me copies of their books and articles and so on....

You obviously went on thinking about the subject because you wrote a series of articles that were published as 'The Image and the Eye',[67] *with the subtitle: 'Further Studies in the Psychology of Pictorial Representation'.*

Yes, I continued to be interested in it. But on the whole, you know, one should not get a wrong impression: I do not read all that much because I write. When one writes, one cannot read.

But, to answer your question, I think it is true that I live not only a double life but a triple life, because of *The Story of Art.*

When I asked you just now about the strange trilogy to whom you pay tribute in the Preface to 'Art and Illusion', I mentioned Köhler, Jakobson and Kokoschka. In the case of Kokoschka, your reasons for citing his influence must be very different from the others?

Kokoschka I mentioned not only out of pride that I knew him, but because he invited me to lecture in Salzburg. He had what he called a 'school of vision' and there he taught amateurs to draw from the model. It was a very interesting experience for me. That was the link with *Art and Illusion*: how immensely important for him the actual momentary act of vision was. He always told his students: remember that what you see now will never, never come again. You must fix it on the canvas, otherwise it will be lost!

Did you know him very well?

Fairly well. Well enough for him not only to invite me to Salzburg, but later to ask me to write the introduction to his great retrospective when he was seventy.

Did you meet him in London?

Yes, he lived in London. Actually, I met him only after the war. But we were fairly often together and he was always very kind to me. He gave me a lithograph of his self-portrait which hangs in my study. When he died, his widow asked me to pronounce his obituary at the Order *pour le mérite* ceremony in Bonn.

Do you like him as a painter?

At his best, he is wonderful, but like so many modern artists he was not very self-critical. He thought: If I do it, it must be good. That is this false theory of art, the theory of self-expression. He was immensely talented and some of his landscapes are wonderful. But he could also be rather careless because he believed in spontaneity. I do not believe at all in spontaneity. But he did. And therefore I don't think that every one of his works is very good. But he was a very fascinating person. He was full of stories and ideas.

Kokoschka was one of my contacts with living art. Of course I have known many other artists and have written prefaces to very many exhibition catalogues of contemporaries.

Do you take much interest in modern art?

Of course I do! How could a historian of art fail to be interested in the transformations of art in the 20th century? I have written chapters about these developments in *The Story of Art* and also several lectures and essays such as 'The Idea of Progress', 'Psychoanalysis and the History of Art', 'The Vogue of Abstract Art' (printed in *Meditations on a Hobby Horse*), 'Image and Word in 20th-Century Art' (in the volume *Topics of our Time*), as well as essays on Kokoschka, on Picasso's Cubism, on Cartier-Bresson, and on the poster artist Abram Games, all in the same volume.

I should like to make a distinction of some importance between the ideology of modern art and the works of modern artists. I am very critical of the ideology of modern art, that is, of the cult of progress and of the *avant garde* which I have frequently analysed and discussed in my chapters on Hegel[68] and elsewhere, in *Ideals and Idols* and in *Tributes*. I agree with Popper that this ideology is intellectually bankrupt and that it has sometimes done harm to art.

But just as I can admire artists of the past whose ideology I do not share, I am also very ready to admit that artists of enormous talent lived in our century. I can admire their inventiveness and their creations. Picasso is an obvious example, but so is Braque or Paul Klee or, among minor masters, Vasarely or others I mentioned in *The Story of Art*. I am even convinced that their search for alternative functions of the visual image after the triumph of photography was justified and produced works of genuine interest.

Who are the modern artists that you love?

I have already mentioned Picasso. I would not say that I always *love* him but I frequently admire his versatility, his wit, and his sheer mastery of form.

Personally I was much closer to Oskar Kokoschka, whom I have mentioned already, and I have always admired and loved Morandi and works by Manzù and Marino Marini. These of course are masters who rejected the ideology of the *avant garde* but surely they belong to this century.

You have written introductions for several exhibition catalogues. For which artists?

I have written introductions to catalogues for many contemporaries who were my friends or whose requests seemed to me worthy of respect. Among them, Oskar Kokoschka must come first. As I've already mentioned, I wrote the introduction to the catalogue of his London retrospective, and I also wrote two introductions to collections of his graphic work, another for his late paintings, for the Marlborough Gallery, and a few others....

I had a dear friend in Switzerland, Max Hunziker, a master of stained-glass paintings and graphic art and oils. When he received the Kulturpreis of the City of Zürich I pronounced his eulogy. This was published, as were my introduction to his major retrospective and other articles.

I knew Gerhart Frankl, an Austrian painter exiled in England, and wrote an introduction to his first posthumous exhibition and another piece for an exhibition in Austria.

Through my sister I knew the daughter of Gustav Mahler, Anna Mahler, and was proud to be asked by her to contribute to a book about her work. I also spoke at her graveside and my few words were published in the second edition.

I also knew the excellent exiled sculptor from Prague, Karel Vogel, and introduced a posthumous exhibition. I have already mentioned Cartier-Bresson and the piece I wrote for his Edinburgh exhibition. Another photographer for whom I wrote an intruduction was Vasco Ascolini, of Reggio Emilia. Among artists active in London whose work I recommended in introductions of varying length I should like to mention Oliver Bevan (who showed abstract mobiles), John Bratby, Milein

Cosman, Barbara Dorf, Abram Games, Marie-Louise Motesiczky and the sculptor Michael Werner. My introduction to the fish paintings by my friend Stanley Meltzoff has not yet been published, but I hope it will be!

Would it be right to say that you pay close attention to what is happening in contemporary art?

Well, of course I pay attention in a general way, but I do not go to many exhibitions arranged by the London galleries. I receive invitations to many of them, but 'art is long and life is short'. I must ration my time! But it sometimes happens that I am much impressed by a catalogue which is sent to me and that I regret my inability to find out more of what happens in art today. It is precisely because I do not believe in the ideology of the *avant garde* that I am convinced that there are many good artists working in many different idioms who form a kind of 'underground' of art, making a modest living without attracting the attention of the media. One can only wish them luck and much satisfaction from what they are doing!

5

THE SENSE OF ORDER

You have often mentioned the name of Karl Popper. This is perhaps the moment to talk about him at more length, before we come to 'The Sense of Order', the book which, with 'Art and Illusion', shows his influence most clearly. Did you know him in Vienna?

Hardly at all. True, I had heard people speak of Popper and I knew that he had written on philosophy. We had acquaintances in common. And actually, it so happened that my father, who was a lawyer, was apprenticed to his father. But I only met him once in Vienna. He came to our house after a concert by the pianist Rudolf Serkin, who was a close mutual friend.

I saw him again in the spring of 1936 in London. At that time he was a schoolteacher in Vienna, but had obtained leave to accept an invitation to England. Somebody had suggested that he should contact me. He lived very near where I lived in Paddington, and we saw much of each other. He was invited by Hayek to give a seminar at the London School of Economics, where I also went. So I heard the lecture which later became *The Poverty of Historicism.* He then returned to Austria to his school-teaching. Then when I went back to Vienna in the autumn of 1936 to finish the book on caricature with Ernst Kris and to get married, we went to see him and his wife.

Some time later, he accepted a lectureship at the University of Canterbury, in New Zealand – that was still before the Nazis came to power. We saw him in London, where he spent two or three days on his way to New Zealand. So I knew him pretty well, and I remember writing to him when I began to work for the BBC, but we did not have a great deal of contact because he was so far away.... And then, in May 1943, I got a letter from Popper, telling me that he had written a book, *The Open Society and its Enemies*. He wanted me to read the manuscript and if I liked it to give it to Professor Hayek. So I read it and was very impressed. I made an appointment with Professor Hayek, in his club in London (this was still during the war), and he gave it to Herbert Read who worked for Routledge, the publishers. He wrote to me asking for a little more information about Popper.

Anyhow, the book was accepted, but Popper, being what he is, started rewriting it. He asked me to help to incorporate his corrections in the manuscript. And for months (this was a time when, to save money, letters were photographed on microfilms) I got these tiny reproductions and I was asked to make changes to various chapters.... I kept all these ninety-five letters I received over a period of sixteen months. Of course, we were then in very close correspondence. There were a few funny incidents, because of the war. One day I telegraphed to him because it was becoming clear that the book was getting too big for one volume and Routledge wanted to divide it into two. So I sent him a telegram saying: 'Routledge suggest division after Chapter 10.' A few hours later I was called back to the post office. The police wanted me to explain what 'division' meant. The censor found the word suspicious. They thought it might be a military division.

Well, in the end, it was really done and sent to the printer. Popper was then invited by Hayek to accept a readership at the London School of Economics. And he came very shortly after the war was over. It was in 1945 or early '46, and we collected him and his wife from the boat, and they stayed with us in our house for a while. We have been on very close terms ever since. We usually talk on the telephone several times a week.

When he came to England to teach at the London School of Economics, he also suggested it might interest me to go to some of his lectures, and I followed his lecture course on logic. Of course we also had many talks about his philosophy. I know little about his philosophy of physics, his ideas about quantum theory and so on. But I was very interested in his interpretation of Plato.... And, in particular, I was very happy when I read the first edition of *The Poverty of Historicism*, which appeared in the journal which Hayek published, to see that he too had so many objections to the idea of 'the spirit of the age'. Here our ideas coincided. The really important thing that I learned from him was the methodological principle, that you can refute a theory but never prove one.

Popper's work is very much present in all your books. In fact, one could say it is your main theoretical reference.

Popper has been much attacked and some of his important ideas have also been adopted by others without acknowledgment, which naturally hurt him a good deal. So I decided that I should stress my debt to Popper whenever I can.

Yes, but it is not just a matter of quoting him. You take from him some of your main methodological principles and some of your main concepts. The 'logic of situation', for example.

You are right. I owe him a great deal. Particularly in psychology. Because, strangely enough, psychologists do not cite him, but he started with psychology. His doctoral thesis was about the psychology of thinking. Let me recall the sentence which I quote at the beginning of the first chapter of *The Sense of Order*:

'It was first in animals and children, but later also in adults, that I observed the immensely powerful *need for regularity* – the need which makes them seek regularities.'[69]

...That is indeed very important and it was from him that I learned it.

That was the starting point for your analysis of decoration which was taken up in 'The Sense of Order'.

Yes, certainly.

That book makes clear your deep interest in psychology, since its subtitle is 'A Study in the Psychology of Decorative Art'.

It is an attempt, perhaps a rather naive attempt, to apply information theory to decoration. What it says, very briefly, is that it is always a break in the order which attracts our attention. But you can have a number of breaks in the order and in that case you get another order at a different level. There is always a tension between the expected redundancies of continuity, and the new step in order or disorder which attracts our attention. This is a slightly complicated theory, so naturally it has not become as well-known as 'schema and correction'.

Your book starts with a description: your gaze was suddenly arrested by the frame round a picture by Raphael, and you asked yourself what function that frame was fulfilling.

To start from this example was purely a matter of presentation.

Not just that. It is quite striking, in a way, that after reading your book, we see the frames which we did not notice before. So, the question is: why do we need a decorated frame around a painting?

We don't need it. But it makes it much easier to look because we know where to stop our eye movements.

But why all those scrolls, all those angels, on the frames?

It is a form of praise, a way of showing how precious the picture is! The frame creates a kind of emphasis. You don't have to look at it, it is still an emphasis, by contrast. The frame contrasts completely with the picture by Raphael. So it is a tremendous break between, on the one hand, the whole museum and, on the other, the picture itself. Of course there are many different types of frame and I don't say that this is a complete explanation. It is just one of the things one can say about it.

What is very interesting in this book is that you show that decoration too has a history. It is a kind of 'story of art', but of 'unregarded art'. The history of the motifs, but also the history of how people react to these motifs.

It is a history of motifs and a history of theories of aesthetics. And that makes it a little more difficult to read, don't you think? It is polyphonic. There are too many things in that book. And it is too long a book, and people no longer read long books.

You often stress in the prefaces of your different books that people don't read books.

Isn't it true?

I don't know. I am not quite sure that nobody reads books.

Maybe some people do. I think young people today read less because of television. My grandson, who reads a great deal of philosophy, tells me that his friends consider reading to be an 'unsocial activity'; you isolate yourself with a book instead of staying with your friends.

Don't you read books?

I do not often read a book from beginning to end. If you ask me to swear how many books I have read last year from cover to cover.... If I review a book I read it, and I wrote a lot of reviews, notably for the *New York Review of Books.* (They have been collected by R. Woodfield under the title *Reflections on the History of Art*).[70]

To go back to your 'too long book', it seems to me that a reader is bound to ask how you arrived at the idea of writing on such a subject. Your Viennese background must play a major role here too.

I say in my introduction that I wrote the book partly because I was annoyed that people thought I was only interested in representation. But that is only a superficial reason. Actually, I was invited to give another series of lectures in the States and I had already given some lectures on ornament in Cambridge.

I also tell in the introduction of that book how my mother collected peasant embroideries of Slovakia. I was very fond of these, and often wondered as a child why people did not consider them to be art. And so I thought it is a very neglected subject. It was not at all neglected in the 19th century. Many people wrote about design and decoration. But in our century this interest has almost totally evaporated. Now it is coming in a little again.

The third reason, and it is an important reason, is Alois Riegl. He had written a book called *Stilfragen* on the history of the acanthus motif, and that I had studied as a student.

So I had every reason to turn to this problem. And I am terribly bored by my colleagues in art history, who always write about the same thing. So, I try to think of things which not everybody has done.

Why did this interest in decoration vanish in our century? Why did it become an 'unregarded' art, as you call it in your Introduction?

One of the reasons is, I think, that there was a kind of tension between abstract art and decoration. You often hear people say, looking at a work of abstract art: 'That would look nice as a curtain.' In other words, it looks like decoration. But the abstract painters don't want to produce decoration, they want to produce High Art. For that reason, abstract art has been anxious to distance itself from decoration. So decoration was pushed away from the centre of interest. It really is an 'unregarded art'. Many people do not notice the patterns of wallpapers or materials.

So when you wrote this book, we can say that this was a new field of research, at least in our century?

Yes, it was entirely new. And my purpose was to put it on the map.

And to make people start noticing it, 'to take it into consideration'.

Absolutely. And, you see, in one sense, I was very fortunate, and I cannot complain. Two of my colleagues in the British Museum, one the keeper of Islamic art, and the other of Chinese art, were very excited by the book. They organized exhibitions and wrote in the catalogues that they owed their interest and inspiration to that book. I was also recently given a 'Diploma of Honour' by the mayor of Faenza (the birthplace of faience) because, as he told me, *The Sense of Order* had been such an inspiration to their school of ceramics.

But psychologists have been a little slow in discussing it. And maybe they are right. Possibly it is both somewhat amateurish and overambitious. I introduce there a kind of metaphorical or mechanical model of how I imagine that our mind works in shifting attention towards awareness of breaks in the order, as I have just said. It is a fact, let us say, that a pilot in a plane does not have to attend to the noise of the engine unless it changes. What he notices is the change. We are constantly monitoring for change. If I pay attention all the time to everything happening in this room, I cannot exist. But if this wall suddenly collapsed, I'd notice it straight away. And this is really the basis of my theory. It is again a kind of Popperian theory, because it is the negative of the expectation, the unexpected, which registers in our mind. More exactly, it is the degree of unexpectedness. In decoration there is a constant interplay between expectation and surprise. This also applies to music; the interplay between the expected and the unexpected, the order of the expected, of the harmonic system, and the deviations and the modulations, diverging from what is expected and then returning to it with the expected cadence....

I was very happy when I learned that there is a form of electro-cardiogram which monitors the heartbeats of people who are in danger. But as this is very expensive, they have invented a machine which does not register the heartbeat all the time, but only when there is a radical change in the rhythm, for instance suddenly much faster. The machine not only records that, but it remembers how it was before, it harks back. And I think that this is precisely how we function: when we notice a change, we can remember what has changed, how it was before.

Where did your interest in information theory come from?

Again, I must give the name of a pioneer of the theory of information, called Colin Cherry, who was an electrical engineer. He wrote a book called *On Human Communication.*[71] I knew him quite well, and we also had discussions. It was from him that I learned the elements of information theory, that is to say that the expected is redundant. When you have a closed system you can mathematically express how many bits of information are needed to convey a particular message.

How did you meet Colin Cherry?

There is a nice institution, here in England, called Cumberland Lodge in Windsor Great Park where university teachers and undergraduates can meet for informal week-end conferences devoted to a variety of topics. I think I met Colin Cherry there. I also met Peter Medawar who became a very great friend. These meetings were a great inspiration when good people came and talked.

This little injection of information theory came from there. Of course, Roman Jakobson also had something to do with my interest.

You said that one of your main sources of inspiration was Riegl's 'Stilfragen'. Could you tell us a little bit more about this book?

As I said, my teacher Julius von Schlosser used to give three kinds of seminars: every fortnight he had one on Vasari and the sources of Vasari, because that was his main field. That was routine. Then he had one in the museum, about the particular pieces that interested him. That is how I got to be interested in medieval ivory carvings. And he had a third kind of seminar, about every two weeks, about theoretical problems or books that had interested him. In the 1930s he decided that it was time somebody looked again at the old book by Alois Riegl, *Stilfragen*, which came out in 1891. He suggested, or I volunteered, I do not remember, that I should give a talk in his seminar on that book, which describes the history of plant ornaments in ancient Egypt and the development of the acanthus motif in Greece. Luckily, Schlosser's seminars were very slow. So you had a lot of time, because between the time when he commissioned you to do it and when you actually had to deliver it, many months might pass. So I began to be very interested in acanthus and – this was perhaps the only original thing that I did – I went to the Natural History Museum to see what acanthus really looks like.

I soon became absolutely obsessed with discovering acanthus everywhere, because the motif is all over the place, in wall papers, in lampshades... everywhere I found acanthus. I was at that time really completely persuaded of the relevance and interest of this approach and of this subject matter. But I did not quite agree with Riegl's methodology. He was a convinced evolutionist and he thought that one could draw a line from the Egyptian lotus to the Greek palmette and from the Greek palmette to the acanthus which then developed into the arabesque like a biological affiliation. I began to doubt this and I said so in my talk. It is true there are forms of the palmette which look a little like acanthus but I would not say that they are necessarily earlier and that the acanthus developed out of the palmette. It may also have been a contamination. I put that also in *The Sense of Order.* So I was critical of the linear development that Riegl postulated, but I thought that the problem he had posed of the continuity of ornament from early Egypt to the Middle Ages was a very important problem. He never followed it up. And nobody has done so since, except those colleagues in the British Museum, whom I mentioned.

Riegl started in the Museum of Applied Art in Vienna, and his first book was about oriental carpets. So this was his introduction to this whole idea of evolution in the arts. There is some evolutionism in my writings too, you know, but he had almost clockwork ideas of the progress of certain tendencies: they *had* to evolve in that way. It was very typical of 19th-century ideas of progress.

What is the link between 'Art and Illusion' and 'The Sense of Order'?

The Sense of Order is not a historical book. It has chapters about history, but also purely thematic chapters, and it has chapters about the history of taste, about the rejection of ornament, about the virtuosity of craftsmen, symbolism, perception.... *Art and Illusion* has basically a chronological theme, the conquest of realism in art, though it also has subsidiary episodes like the development of caricature. That makes it also much easier to read. The real link between the two books is what has always been my ambition, that if one writes about such subjects, one should present an explanatory hypothesis. Both these books put forward hypothetical explanations of phenomena which we encounter when we study the history of art.

Do you think that we can have a rational explanation of what ornament is for?

We have no ultimate explanation, of course. All we can say is that the perception of regularity in abstract forms is a primitive function that is necessary for our survival. Animals too can recognise such regularities: think of bees in their search for flowers. Or of the forms and colours characteristic of animal species. Another man whom I knew and who influenced me very much is Konrad Lorenz.

Were you really very much influenced by Lorenz?

I understand why you ask that question. Let me tell you the

whole story. I had read with great admiration his popular book on animals. And I very much wanted to read a philosophical article that he had written during the war on the necessary limits of human experience. I found that equally interesting – up to the point where he talks of decadence as a danger facing the human race. It seemed to me that his point of view, and the actual formulae that he employed, resembled in a very worrying way the racist arguments of the Nazis when they were talking about the Jews. I was therefore on the point of refusing to participate in a collective volume on forms to which Lorenz was also going to contribute. But in the end, the editor of the book, L.L Whyte reassured me and I gave him my article called 'Meditations on a Hobby Horse'.[72] When I later got to know Lorenz I realized that beyond any possible doubt he was horrified by what the Nazis had done.

One of his best friends in Vienna, a Jew, had gone into hiding in Holland, where he was discovered by the Nazis, arrested and murdered. I met Lorenz at the house of this man's sister. It was quite clear that Lorenz was haunted by what had happened to his friend. He wept. It made me soften in my judgment of him. What I liked was that he said: 'Such a man *we* killed.' He did not say 'they' but 'we'. And this I liked. You may know, too, that he had been a very close friend of Karl Popper in his youth and continued to think highly of him all his life.[73]

And then, one cannot help admiring his deep sympathy with the animals that he studied, and the talent for mimicry that he showed when he was imitating their movements. When he talked, at a conference, about grey geese, he really *became* a grey goose, it was incredible. I am sure that he was one of the great geniuses of our century, and that his discovery of 'imprinting' – how a newborn animal follows the first thing it sees, which is usually its mother – assures him a place in the history of science. I have to add that, in spite of everything, because he was basically a biologist, I suspect he remained a racist all his life. I almost told him so at our last meeting in Vienna, when he expressed the opinion that the Jews were the most intelligent people anywhere. That is still a racist idea.

As a result, I always felt that I should maintain a certain distance. That was not the case with the other great specialist in animal behaviour, Nikko Tinbergen, who lived in Oxford, and with whom my mother, my sister and I formed quite a close friendship.

You must be the only art historian to have been influenced by zoologists.

Yes, because I was interested in the perception of order, in the animal as well as the human world. My approach is always biological. I always try to go back to the beginning.

Your approach is both psychological and biological?

Well, psychology is biology.

But isn't it a problem to mix up cultural explanations, biological explanations, sociological explanations and aesthetic explanations, all in the same book?

It is only a problem of presentation, not of theory. If you are interested in history, you have to face the fact that history has to be chronological: you start with the ancient Egyptians and then go on. And if you are interested in biology or philosophy, in systematic thought, you start with an axiom and then go on and explain it. When you are interested in both, the real literary problem is to find some means of keeping the chronological order without sacrificing the systematic thought. That is the difficulty of *The Sense of Order*, I think – that it did not quite integrate the two. Because there is no history of ornament as there is a history of representation.

One of the points that seem very important to the reader of 'The Sense of Order' is that you make no hierarchical distinction between fine art and applied art, or between primitive and developed art...

I do suggest some hierarchy since I say somewhere that decorative art reached an extraordinary climax at least three times: in Anglo-Irish miniatures (*The Book of Kells*), in Muslim arabesque (the Alhambra) and in Rococo interiors (Bavarian churches). You could add flamboyant Gothic. You do sometimes find such a development of a decorative style to great sophistication and richness. And usually that leads to a point when people get tired of it and want to start again. That is an observation made long ago by the great medievalist Prosper Merimée.[74]

But my question was not about the hierarchy within the decorative arts, but about the hierarchy between different kinds of art, levels of art. You show that the decorative arts may be just as rewarding for the art historian as any other form of art.

In that respect I would not say that I was very original. When I said just now that *The Sense of Order* represented a new area of research for the 20th century, I did not mean, obviously, that historians of art and architecture had never studied the forms of decoration specific to each period. Focillon in France, with *La vie des formes*, was very interested in flamboyant styles; and Fiske Kimball did some remarkable work on the origins of Rococo.

You quote in your book a very interesting anecdote: a discussion you had with Panofsky as to whether the style of an altar painting and the architecutral decoration around it both expressed the same, unique artistic style.

Yes, I asked him: 'Do you think that 'the Gothic style' really exists?' And he said: 'Yes.'

It is a very important matter: if he is right, it means that there are styles which embrace everything that happens within a particular period.

Yes, of course it is a very important matter! And I say in the book that I have a bit of bad conscience when I pronounce an opinion on this point, because sometimes what you say is true and sometimes it is not. What I maintain is that there are certainly moments, like the Rococo, which go very far in general preference for certain forms, such as lightness, grace and playfulness.[75] We all know frames of mirrors or Rococo pictures which are decorated in an asymmetrical and extravagant style. But there are also contrary examples: the frames round Velazquez's paintings, for instance, do not harmonize in this way with the formal treatment of the paintings themselves. And since, above all, in my view, Rococo has all the characteristics of a fashion, it is evident that this bias did not affect everything that was produced at this period. The same goes for all styles and all periods. It is we who project upon the continuous flux of history such categories as 'Mannerism', and it is evident that not everybody at that period was a Mannerist.

This may seem a minor disagreement, but if you were to question me about Panofsky, I would have to say that the disagreement was just the tip of the iceberg.

In fact, it is his whole way of envisaging the history of styles and of history itself which is at issue in this discussion.

To put it briefly, Panofsky represented a German tradition of art history which I have often criticized. It is a tradition that goes back, as I have tried to show, to Hegel's philosophy of history and which loves to operate with ideas of the *Zeitgeist* (spirit of the age) and *Volksgeist* (spirit of the people).[76] This tradition postulates that all the manifestations of an era – philosophy, art, social structures, etc. – must be considered as expressions of an essence, an identical spirit. As a result, every era is considered as a totality embracing everything. A great deal of erudition and ingenuity has been exercised by art historians of this persuasion to demonstrate interconnections of this sort. Panofsky, with his intelligence and outstanding knowledge, also loved to establish these links. I remember that he wrote that Michelangelo's drawing technique corresponded exactly to his Neoplatonism. And, as you know, he devoted a book to this kind of connection: his study of Gothic architecture and scholasticism.[77]

Right at the beginning of his book *Renaissance and Renascences in Western Art*,[78] in the first chapter, called 'Renaissance: self-definition or self-deception', he takes up the old idea that the Renaissance was the expression of a specific 'spirit'. In one of the footnotes he refers to a criticism of this theory made by my friend George Boas, the historian and philosopher.[79] Boas had objected that one could not define historical periods as one defines animal species. Panofsky replied, politely but firmly, that, in his opinion, one could. He explained that there was a difference between a statement such as: 'Cats are distinguished from dogs by embodying the spirit of cathood, as opposed to that of doghood,' and a statement such as: 'Cats are distinguished from dogs by a combination of characteristics (such as the possession of retractable claws, ... and the inability to swim...) which, in the aggregate, describe the *genus Felis* as opposed to the *genus Canis.*' And Panofsky added: 'Should someone decide, for the sake of convenience, to designate the sum total of such characteristics as "cathood" and "doghood", it would do violence to the English language, but not to method.'[80]

When I came across an article in the *Times* of 18 December

1964, on cats which could swim, I cut it out and sent it to George Boas... but not to Panofsky.

This Aristotelian idea of 'essence of cathood' or 'essence of the Renaissance' is precisely what Boas and I do not accept. But Panofsky believed in it absolutely. I remember an art historical congress in Amsterdam in 1952. People were beginning to be a little critical of Jacob Burckhardt and the idea of the Renaissance, and that made Panofsky very cross. He put on the screen two different buildings, a Renaissance church and a Gothic church, and he said: 'Something must have happened.' And I said to myself: 'Of course something happened, they introduced a new style of architecture. But this is not necessarily the symptom of something else.'

You recently gave a talk on Panofsky....

Yes, in fact, I have criticized Panofsky, not only in the passage which you mention in *The Sense of Order*, but also in a lecture which has now been published, where I talk about Panofsky's book called *Idea.*[81] It was a rather critical lecture, because although I admire him very much, he was guilty of forcing the evidence. He was very skillful in dialectics, and immensely intelligent, and he enjoyed presenting his case like a lawyer. But he often went too far. He knew it and could laugh at himself. He used to say: 'Beware of the boa constructor.'

Let me ask you a more specific factual question. Panofsky had been very close to Aby Warburg and the Institute....

Yes, when they were both in Hamburg. Panofsky was a Professor of Art History at the University of Hamburg. People always believe that he was a member of the staff of the Warburg Institute in Hamburg. He was not. He had his professorship in the University – the Warburg Institute was separate. But he was on very close terms with Warburg (who died in 1929) and with Saxl, the new director, with whom he wrote a book on Dürer's *Melancholia*.

But in that case, why did he not join the Warburg Institute when it migrated to London?

Well, they were very close, and if you want to know the whole truth, he was a little hurt, or perhaps more than a little hurt, that when the Warburg moved to London, he was not invited also to come. But Saxl had his reasons: he thought Panofsky had a good job in America and he ought first to look after all these people who had no jobs.... But I know from Mrs Panofsky that he was a little hurt.

Why is there no article on Panofsky in 'Tributes', the volume in which you pay homage to the 'interpreters of our cultural tradition', as you put it in the subtitle?

Because I did not know him well enough.

Yes, but you read him, and that should have been enough for you to have paid homage. Did you in fact feel so remote from him that it seemed difficult to pay homage? After all, you were able to write well enough about Hegel in that volume! [82]

I should like to insist – and this is very important to me – that the differences in our approaches, and other differences about which we should speak later, never for an instant cast a shadow over the cordiality of our relations. Every time, or almost every time, that I went to America I used to visit this great and admired scholar. And I was always touched by the warmth of his welcome and his hospitality. And I have kept many generous letters from him in which he thanks me for having sent him my publications.

But to answer your question, let me refer to the obituary that I wrote for *The Burlington Magazine*.[83] In that article I related that he once said to me: 'There are people who are conceited, and there are people who are vain. I may be vain, but I am not conceited.' And this was true. He liked praise and he was a little vain. But he did not think that he was wonderful. He also had a genuine modesty. He was so successful in America, he was a kind of divinity. But precisely because he was so privileged he felt obliged to help younger colleagues. He was very generous with his time.

It is a matter for regret that the almost unchallenged dominance that he enjoyed over art history during his lifetime has led today to a rather ungenerous reaction, completely misjudging the qualities of an art historian who was capable of writing such a masterpiece as his monograph on Dürer.

There are many differences between Panofsky and yourself. But there is one which seems particularly striking: we can speak of a Panofskian method, but I do not have the feeling that we can speak of a Gombrichian method. Your prefaces never include a statement of 'the rules of historical method' – if we except certain general principles derived from Popper, which we have already discussed. Can we say that you have no method?

I don't want one. I just want common sense! This is my only method.

What do you mean?

Well, it is quite simple: we ask a question and try to find out how it can be answered. There are many questions in history we cannot answer, because there is no evidence. There are so many things we cannot know. I always say that history is like a Swiss cheese, there are many holes in it. The skill of the historian consists precisely in finding questions to which he thinks he may get an answer. Before you do any research, you have to decide what questions to ask. The skill, one could say the tact, of the scholar, is to have a feeling that this or that line of inquiry is promising, that you may find out something. Because, as I say, in many cases, the result is: 'maybe, maybe not'.

But to ask a question, you need a method. It is no good asking naïve questions.

Yes, you are absolutely right, but every question demands a different method to answer it. I always say: 'If you want to drive in a nail, you use a hammer, and if you want to put in a screw, you use a screwdriver.' So you must know which method you apply for which question. There are many questions in history for which the best method will be to go to the archives and see whether there is a document that gives the answer. Is there a document to tell us when this painting was painted and who commissioned it? These are methods of course: searching, what people call 'research', looking for evidence, for answers.

There are other things, let us say the subject-matter of a picture, where the answer may be in a text. Then you have to know which text to look for and make the connection. If it is an astrological cycle, for instance, you have to try to find the relevant text and if you are lucky, you find it. All these things are what I call common sense: a sort of intuition about where you can look for either an explanation or an answer. There is no method, in the sense that you can apply the same kind of search to everything.

But it seems to me that there is a kind of common factor, if I can put it that way, in your method of tackling problems.

Certainly. But perhaps there is one more thing to be said: nothing – in art history or history of philosophy – exists in a void. You do not start from scratch, but from what other people have done – you answer to what has been said already. It is like a telephone conversation. You say: 'That cannot be true,' and you go on from there. There is always a strong body of traditional opinion. In that sense, most of my papers are responses to some accepted position, or an idea that I was critical about. Let us say Panofsky's ideas about Gothic, or whatever else. One is constantly in dialogue with other colleagues.

I have written an article on the *Stanza della Segnatura* by Raphael where I said that I do not believe that Raphael had very much advice from learned scholars to construct the symbolism of these paintings. I tried to show that most of it one could explain by the tradition of earlier pictures in the Vatican.[84] The same is true of the Sistine ceiling. These artists knew of course what their colleagues had done, and the tradition in which they had worked, and they incorporated certain modifications of their own. But they did not need a learned man by their side to tell them that God created the world or that Apollo was the leader of the Muses. My article on the *Stanza della Segnatura* is therefore a criticism of those who believed that they did. So is, for instance, my article on Hieronymus Bosch. I found in reading the *Historia Scholastica*, a kind of narrative based on the Bible, you could explain much of *The Garden of Earthly Delights*.[85]

Is an interpretation therefore always a contribution to a controversy?

Yes, one is trying to propose a solution that is better than somebody else's. For example, in *Symbolic Images* there is an article on the Palazzo del Tè of Giulio Romano. It is one of my safest interpretations. It arose because an article on the frescoes of the Palazzo del Tè had been submitted to the *Journal of the Warburg and Courtauld Institutes* and I was asked to read it. It seemed to me totally unconvincing. I said to myself: 'Surely I can find a better solution than this.' So even that was, in a sense, part of a controversy.[86]

At other times it is just a matter of chance: one reads a book, and suddenly one thinks of a picture. For instance, my article on the *Orion* by Poussin.[87] I don't think I was looking for the answer. I was reading Natalis Comes about mythologies; I read this story and I suddenly thought: 'Remember Poussin.'

So 'the logic of discovery' is a matter of luck?

Well, let's say it's more a matter of reading. If you never read a book, it will not happen to you.

Yes, I was just wondering: how do you choose the subject matter of your articles? Why this painting or this problem and not another one?

First of all, as I have said, most of my articles were lectures first. So you have to go a step back and ask: 'Why do you select this or that topic for a lecture?' I think, for instance, in the case of Raphael, I had been lecturing in Oxford about drawing, and I mentioned these first drawings by Raphael for the *Stanza*, and later I developed my ideas into another lecture and then developed them again.... Sometimes an invitation stipulates that you have to lecture on a particular picture. That was the case for my lecture on the *Madonna della Sedia*.[88] But it does not quite answer your question. One has a certain feeling about certain problems. It is a kind of give and take. For example, I had always been interested in Leonardo and I often read and re-read Leonardo's writings. I had to compile the index to the Richter edition of Leonardo's writings; I know his writings pretty well, and I return to them very often. So when I was invited to talk at Vinci to commemorate his birthday, I knew what subject to take.[89]

So I think it may be true, if you go through my articles, that quite a number come from reading or teaching and remembering pictures.

Of course, one has some ideas which go through one's whole life. A kind of '*idée fixe*'.

PART THREE

The Urge to Explain

6

THE LIMITS OF INTERPRETATION

You have written a lot of articles to give your interpretations on paintings, frescoes and pictorial cycles and you gathered a number of these papers in four volumes of 'Studies in the Renaissance'.[90] *It seems true to say that the Renaissance is the period to which you have devoted the major part of your historical work.*

As a historian of art, certainly. And of the Renaissance, mainly (not only, but mainly) the 15th century.

This interest in the Renaissance goes back a long way. You wrote about Giulio Romano, when you were still in Vienna.

Yes, it was my doctoral thesis, as I told you. But this interest also owes an enormous amount to the Warburg Institute. There are two aspects to it. Aby Warburg's own centre of interest was the circle of Lorenzo de' Medici. So when I went to Florence after the war, I also did some work in archives and libraries on some members of a family, the Sassetti, who commissioned works of art. I never published the results of that research. It would mean a huge amount of further work in the archives, because it is about a conflict between the monastery of Vallombrosa and the Curia. I found very soon that I could not do this work without really sitting in Italy for a long time. But I still think somebody should do it.[91]

Anyhow, as I told you, Warburg wrote his dissertation on Botticelli and then wrote about Ghirlandaio and other masters of the late Quattrocento. So, since I was working on Warburg's papers I read a good deal about that period and the debates about the Renaissance. While in Vienna everybody talked about Mannerism, but at the Warburg Institute everyone talked about Neoplatonism. It was the great intellectual fashion of that time. Raymond Klibansky and Edgar Wind were no longer in London, but Rudolf Wittkower was interested in Platonism in architectural theory, and Frances Yates was studying the esoteric currents of the Renaissance which had influenced Giordano Bruno. And D. P. Walker knew all there was to know about music and magic in the Renaissance. So I got interested too and I read Ficino. I remember reading his correspondence and coming across a letter which I thought would help to explain the *Primavera*. I'm no longer so sure, but at that time I thought so. And that was the beginning of my work on Botticelli: the link between Neoplatonism and Botticelli's 'mythologies'.[92]

Can you remind us in a few words what your interpretation was?

I mentioned a letter by Ficino to Lorenzo de' Medici's cousin Lorenzo di Pierfrancesco, the patron of Botticelli, who was then a young man. In that letter Ficino offers a kind of symbolic horoscope and exhorts young Lorenzo to love Venus, who represents *Humanitas*. He also insists that the young man should learn this letter by heart. I suggested that the painting of Venus and the Graces, the so-called *Primavera*, was intended to keep this lesson before the eyes of the young man and to influence his character. I quoted a good many texts to support this possibility and also suggested that for the representation of Venus Botticelli was advised to use a description of her in *The Golden Ass* by Apuleius. I still believe that this hypothesis is very plausible but few colleagues now agree with me. It would make the *Primavera* into an almost religious didactic composition rather than a pagan illustration. But it is hard to prove.

Your hypothesis was not well received?

A certain number of people thought I was right. Others did not. There are a few things which make my hypothesis a little less likely. At that time, we all believed that the picture came from Castello, the villa of Lorenzo di Pierfrancesco. Now, it appears that it was in his palazzo in Florence. To some extent the chain of events I had tried to reconstruct in my article was therefore broken. I wrote a kind of postscript for a new edition of *Symbolic Images*.[93] I cannot accuse myself of having concealed the contrary evidence.

But at that time, for a year or more, I was completely steeped in the ideas about Neoplatonism, just as André Chastel was at that time. We were both working on this idea. He then published his book on Ficino and art.[94] Panofsky had started it all: he had two chapters on Ficino in his *Studies in Iconology*. At that time, after the war, when I returned from my work with the BBC, I plunged into these studies in Neoplatonism. And I also taught it: when I gave my classes for historians at the Warburg Institute, one term was always devoted to the revival of Platonism in the Renaissance. I am not a historian of philosophy, but I knew some of the texts, and I read them with my students in Latin.

Botticelli is one thing. But then I became interested in a more general topic connected with Neoplatonism. You will find it in my article on 'Icones Symbolicae'.[95] It developed from an old idea of mine: in Austria, there are many Baroque frescoes, allegorical ceiling paintings representing *The Seven Virtues*, *The Liberal Arts*, or whatever else, all floating in the clouds! I once gave a lecture in Vienna (one of my very first) in which I suggested that there was not much difference between personifications like those of Faith and so on, on the one hand, and angels and saints on the other. If we ever go to Heaven, we shall see not only the saints but also Faith, as a real being, an essence. Now, in turning the pages of a big book by Graevius, a kind of anthology of writings on theology, I came across a sermon by a man called Giarda, *Icones Symbolicae.* It was the sermon he gave in 1626, at the opening of a monastic library which had representations of symbolic images. He suggested (not without rhetorical exaggeration) that these are the true representations of the Virtues. They are Platonic 'ideas' in Heaven. This was the origin of a paper I read at Oxford University in which I asked what is the status of these personifications: are they representations or not? (That links it with *Art and Illusion.*) And I suggested that for a Platonist they are representations. But what about for an Aristotelian? For him, they also represent an essence, but they are much more like the intellectual definition of the subject. I tried to follow two trends: the more mystical trend of Neoplatonism, and the more rational, scholastic one, in order to explain the different approaches to personification. I think it is probably one of the more difficult papers I have written. I don't know how much of it is completely right. But it was an important attempt to clarify what one might call the status of the visual image. What did the painter mean when he painted *Faith*, or *Charity,* on a wall? Might we be influenced by the emanations of these figures? Could one experience a kind of mystical union while meditating on these figures?

This links with the whole question of religious images in the Christian Church. According to the Ten Commandments we are not allowed to represent God. So they had to say: 'Well, yes and no… this image is not a representation of the Divine, but the Church must accommodate itself to our limited intellect....' This is the doctrine of 'accommodation'. We find the same thing in Dante. He said: 'Of course, it is not a real picture of God, but the Church has to talk in these terms.'

Your mind cannot be taught in other ways
Because it only grasps the sensory
And later suits it to the intellect.

That is the reason why the Holy Writ
Adjusts its language to your comprehension
Ascribing hand and feet to God, but never means it.

And our Holy Church doth represent
St Michael and St Gabriel as humans
No less than him who restored health to Tobit.[96]

This is a very central question for the history of art. Because in a way, for the naive mind, or the mystical mind, it is unthinkable that the personifications are just signs like the letter A. They are more than that. But exactly what? This is partly a psychological, and partly a philosophical question. In my criticism of Panofsky's *Idea*[97] I wondered whether I may have been a little too schematic in dividing Platonism from Aristotelianism. Most people were not interested in the technical questions of philosophers. There is much more syncretism. Everything comes together in one great experience. Many of these painters, or even educated men, did not mind very much whether their ideas were more Platonic or more Aristotelian. It was the wisdom of the ancients and that was enough for them!

Even so, I think that the question of what exactly an image stands for is immensely interesting. My son teaches Sanskrit at Oxford but his main interest is Buddhism. Everybody knows one thing about the Buddha: that he attained Nirvana, and in that sense he no longer exists. Nevertheless, you go on praying in front of a Buddha statue. What the status of this statue is is not so obvious. But then, we are not always logical in our approach to these questions. Maybe we are making a mistake if we try to be too logical.

You think the art historian must be careful not to be too logical?

Yes, he must not project his own logic on the mind of the period that he is studying. When it comes to religion, people are not so logical.

The collection that contains your article 'Icones Symbolicae' is called 'Symbolic Images'. It implies that you were then involved in iconographic and iconologic researches. But today, it seems to me, you feel more cautious about iconology.

That book was, let us say, the most Warburgian of my works. The introduction, which I called 'The aims and limits of iconology',[98] was written last, of course, and I was able to step back from it a bit and to criticize some of the implications of iconology which derived from Panofsky. But Panofsky himself was very unhappy about his own influence on iconology. He once told a friend of mine that when a new number of the *Art Bulletin* appeared, he always dreaded what parodies of his own method there might be in it.

You mean scholars trying to discover symbolism behind everything in a painting?

Yes, in my introduction to *Symbolic Images* I tried to make some methodological recommendations. I said, for instance, that one should never construct an interpretation if one could not refer, not just to vague similarities to a text, but also to other well documented examples. Otherwise the interpretation remains completely up in the air.

Let me tell you about the one public disagreement that I had with Panofsky. As I said, when I went to Princeton, I always visited him. One one occasion, he had on his table a lot of photographs of the frescoes by Correggio in the Camera di San Paolo at Parma. He said he had a new interpretation and he would be happy if we would publish it (I was director of the Warburg Institute at the time). But he did not want it to be just an article, it must be a whole book. So, I said: 'Of course, let it be a book.' But when he sent the manuscript, I found it quite unconvincing. He tried to show that one could understand all the scenes represented there as allusions to a dispute between the abbess and the Roman Curia. But he admitted that he could not interpret the whole cycle as a coherent statement. As usual, he displayed immense knowledge in his search for a meaning for each image, but I could not call to mind any other similar fresco-cycle where a quarrel of this sort had been used as an excuse for so many erudite allusions. I wrote him a letter in Latin, half as a joke, to say that of course we would print it but that I was almost frightened by the boldness of his ideas. He understood perfectly well. And then I thought of an alternative interpretation, based on the armorial bearings of the abbess, which consisted of three moons. That kind of eulogistic programme seemed to me much more plausible for a decorative scheme, even if I could not prove it.[99]

There is another more important area where I cannot accept Panofsky completely, and that is his ideas about symbolism in Dutch painting of the 15th century. I think he goes too far.

Art historians indeed seem to be turning their backs on that kind of interpretation. I am thinking of Svetlana Alpers' book on 'the art of describing', about Dutch 17*th-century painting, which seems to have been written to* *contradict the way Panofsky and his disciples saw things. She refuses to see any symbolism in Dutch painting, but only a wish to 'describe' the exterior world.*[100]

Well, you know, the Warburg Institute was very much under the influence of Panofsky. But my younger colleagues are rather reluctant to follow his line. They are much more down-to-earth. They don't believe that there is so much symbolism in pictures. So there is a kind of reaction. In fact, perhaps, too much reaction, in the sense that people do not read him any more.

You yourself seem to be rather more than 'reluctant' when it comes to iconological interpretations.

Absolutely. And I see a good deal of it, because I have to read articles sent to the *Journal of the Warburg and Courtauld Institutes.* Sometimes they are completely fantastic.

We spoke a short time ago about the Sistine Chapel and the *Stanza della Segnatura* of Raphael. There is a great heap of learned articles about the meanings to be found in the Sistine ceiling: why this prophet and not another prophet? But, like many others, I have come round to believing what Michelangelo said. He said he had been left free to paint whatever he liked. And what he liked was to follow tradition. There is no reason to believe that the Sistine ceiling has more meanings than what we see. After all, what more do you want than the creation of the world and of man? It can be shown in detail that Michelangelo himself put together all the Old Testament episodes, and that he certainly learned it all by himself, from the tradition that includes the ceiling mosaics of the Florence Baptistery, Ghiberti and Jacopo della Quercia; and that the sybils were an extremely popular theme with painters at this time.... It is quite unnecessary to suppose that scholars had to furnish the programme for him. And as a result, there is no hidden significance to be sought. I have tried to show the same thing with the *Stanza della Segnatura* by Raphael. There are people who believe that every gesture has a definite meaning, based on a programme which learned humanists wrote for Raphael, but in that case how could he make so many changes to the designs? He must have been free to make them. Certainly, he had a general framework for what he intended, which was again based on a tradition. But in doing so he made a composition in his own style. It is a great work of art not because it has so many meanings, but because it is beautiful.

But you yourself have done a lot of research of this kind.

Yes and you can even call 'Icones Symbolicae', my article on Ficino and Neoplatonism, an iconological article. I have written about iconography. In fact, I enjoy it. And I made some contributions which, I think, are still valid: about Bosch, Giulio Romano or Poussin, where I hope to have really solved the problem; I can say: this painting comes from *this* text....

You said just now that your interpretation of the 'Primavera' seems to you now less solid.

I think that is the main example of a case where I have changed my mind. I was wholly absorbed in this problem as you know, and I really thought that I had made a discovery. What began to worry me, and not only me but my colleagues, and even Panofsky, was that it was not at all difficult to find such meanings. On the contrary it was rather too easy. Anybody who studies Renaissance poetry or philosophy is sure to find numerous references to Venus and the Graces. The problem is to know whether they are the texts that the painter illustrated. Yet, I still think that it was not a useless exercise, and that other interpretations of the *Primavera* are even less convincing than my own.

Do you think today that it is really 'too easy' to find the meaning of paintings, which comes down to saying that it is all too likely that you are inventing or making a mistake?

Yes, unless you find a text that corresponds without question.

But it follows that when you are sure that you have discovered a text which inspired a painting, you can then state for certain that without discovering that text we should never have been able to guess or reconstruct the meaning of that picture. Now, this surely makes any hypothesis that we put forward to explain a picture for which we have found no corresponding text extremely uncertain. You have even spoken of 'the elusiveness of meaning'.

That is precisely what I think now.

Surely that leads to an extremely cautious attitude even when we have found a text that seems to correspond?

Well, as a follower of Popper, I think we are always fallible. We can never be quite sure, but there is an approximation to being sure. I briefly referred just now to the article in *Symbolic Images* on the *Sala dei Venti* in the Palazzo del Tè by Giulio Romano, which has an astrological meaning. Now, if there had been only one or two scenes which corresponded with the text, then it would have been very difficult to know whether I was right. But when you go through the text and see that every time what it describes is what is represented on the walls, you no longer have any doubts that the interpretation fits. It is like a detective story: if you have only one clue, maybe somebody else did the murder. But if so many things come together, you can gradually narrow down the margin of error. I personally think, but not everybody agrees with me, that I am right about my interpretation of the *Garden of Earthly Delights* by Hieronymus Bosch. There are too many totally independent pieces of evidence which all converge on this idea that it represents mankind before the flood.

I would not say it is never possible to find out what a particular picture illustrates but the correspondence with the text should not be forced.

It is in the framework of this discussion that you have delivered a very strong criticism of psychoanalytic interpretations. You point out (what seems to me of crucial importance) that 'meaning' is not a subjective psychological notion but must be connected with social and cultural institutions.

Yes, I believe that the vogue for iconology, for interpreting the symbols of the Renaissance, is not unconnected with psychoanalysis. Freud started it up to a point, in his Leonardo paper. But others went much further. I do not say that psychoanalysts are always wrong. But their notion of 'overdetermination' is very problematic. When an artist painted a picture for somebody he would not tell him: 'It means this and this and this.' That might happen today, but not in the Renaissance.

In the Renaissance, the commission is much more important than the feelings of the artist.

Absolutely.

When did the idea originate that art is the expression of the artist's deep sensibility?

Not before the Romantics, at the beginning of the 19th century. There are a lot of good books on this, and the best I know, though it is more about literature than about art, is by M. H. Abrams, called *The Mirror and the Lamp.*[101] It presents a wonderful description of what happened.

Music is the best example. In the 18th century, music was considered to paint 'affects'. Mozart wrote about this in his letters: he wanted to represent the fury of Osmin, or the sadness of Constanze. These are not Mozart's own feelings, but the feelings of the characters in the operas. This is the doctrine of 'affects', of how art can paint or represent the affects, and through the representation can move the spectator. The artist manipulates our response; he asks: how can I best convey sadness or joy? This is part of the classical theory of rhetoric which has always interested me. It is only in the Romantic period that the idea grew up that it would be dishonest of the artist so to work on our emotions. The new ideal of 'sincerity' demanded that he must represent his own feelings.

And the birth of this tradition, you think, was it in Germany or in France?

The great figure is of course Rousseau. 'Sincerity' is a key concept in *Les Confessions*. Of course, he was not very sincere, but he may have believed that he was. But it is also in Goethe, up to a point, in Wordsworth in England, the idea that a poem is nothing but an overflow of feelings.

In a lecture I gave recently at the Royal Academy I talked about this change from the 18th-century idea of decorum, that 'art must be noble', to the idea that came later, that 'art must be sincere'.[102] It is round about 1800 that you find these beliefs very strongly.

So, in the Renaissance period, it is not a matter of self-expression but of…

…creating the right mood. When you write a drama about Bacchus and Ariadne, you must write about how Ariadne feels when she discovers that Bacchus has abandoned her…. It is a famous *topos* of the Renaissance, the 'lament of Ariadne'. You should be able to write it so that everybody is moved.

I think this older idea of the expression of feeling is self-evidently true. If somebody has to write a symphony, he cannot wait till he is cheerful to write the scherzo, and sad to write the adagio. He knows what it is to be sad. He remembers. It is a matter of technical knowledge, of artistic skill.

But, again, with psychoanalysis, this confessional character of art came so much to the fore because art came, through the Romantics, to be identified with dreams.

Freud thought that Leonardo painted Saint Anne because he had two mothers. But Leonardo painted Saint Anne because she was the patron saint of Florence and he had been commissioned to paint Saint Anne.[103] There is a story in Vasari which I believe. When Leonardo came back from Milan to Florence, Filippino Lippi had been commissioned to paint Saint Anne for the town hall of Florence. And when he heard that Leonardo had arrived, he abandoned his commission and gave the job to Leonardo. It sounds an unlikely story, but it is probably true, because when Leonardo had left Florence, Filippino had taken over one of his commissions. Anyhow it is a more likely explanation than that he had two mothers!

But it remains true that all paintings carried out to a similar commission are far from being identical to one another.

Because the whole point was to do better than the others. And to show by this that you were a great artist.

7

MATTERS OF TASTE

I have the impression that your researches into the art of the Renaissance, numerous and important as they are, became rather secondary in your work as a whole.

The fact is that the more I became involved in the Warburg Institute, the less time I had to go to the archives in Florence. But it is not quite true that I entirely abandoned work on Renaissance subjects. I did a little less, but I gave classes at the Warburg Institute, and when I was invited to give lectures, I selected some of these problems I was teaching about. And these lectures you find in my four volumes of essays on the art of the Renaissance. So that I always kept the Renaissance on the boil, so to speak, but on a side-burner. And one of the problems which never left me was Leonardo. Because in Leonardo you also have his interest in science and in perception. I have written a lot on Leonardo.

Is Leonardo among your favourite subjects?

Yes, but I know that one can never finish with him. Leonardo is a miracle and a miracle is inexhaustible.

I said that you had relegated Renaissance studies to the background because it does not seem to me that the quest for new facts about this picture or that picture is what interests you any longer.

I am always pleased when I find a new fact. I was very happy when I found out what Poussin's *Orion* meant. But you are no doubt right: my ambition now goes a little further than that. I had the feeling that the general topics of representation and decoration were too neglected. I was impatient when I found so much detail in the literature and nothing of the more general problems. I still think that we are a little short of more general ideas in our discipline. Of course, the emphasis on general ideas is in itself derived from German and Austrian art history. I did not invent it. The English are by nature very positivist. They want to go into detail and after this great vogue for iconology, they went back to the detailed research, without philosophical background. And I still represent this older tradition that one cannot ask new interesting questions without keeping general problems in mind.

You spoke of your ambition. What is your ambition?

My ambition is to explain. To look at the development of art from a slightly greater distance. To see what is going on there.

Can you give an example of something that you consider did achieve that ambition?

Well, I would say that *Art and Illusion* is this kind of explanation...

And in your Renaissance studies?

In *The Heritage of Apelles*, you will find my study called 'From the Revival of Letters to the Reform of the Arts', in which I try to analyse the transition from the intellectual preoccupation of a small élite to the stylistic movement that we call the Renaissance.[104] Or again, I could mention my reinterpretation of

Mannerism. I do not believe that Mannerism was an expression of a psychological crisis. And there I coined that word which I used as the title of the volume of my French essays, *L'écologie de l'art.* My point of view is more sociological: in the special climate of the Gonzaga Court of Mantua the court painter was obliged to entertain and amuse his lord who was not a very easy man to please. So Giulio Romano had to practise a different kind of art from what Raphael and Michelangelo had done in Rome. Quite apart from Giulio's talents, he knew that he was expected to produce sensational and thrilling effects. I no longer believe that he created these effects as the expression of an inner torment. He knew that he had to amuse all the time: '*Etonnez-moi*,' that was really the situation. When the artist who preceded him at the Gonzaga court was falling from favour, he promised the duke to create new *bizarreries*, such as no one had ever seen before.[105] Alas, Giulio Romano was better at that game.

So you have a certain social ambiance which creates certain expectations of the artist. And one cannot deal with the history of art without dealing with these expectations: novelty... and so on. In our time artists must always create something new. It is what Rosenberg calls 'the tradition of the new'. In the 12th century, nobody wanted something new.

You think that this kind of sociological approach is more rewarding than the iconological one?

They must all come together. But I think one cannot neglect the question, what is the function of an image, the social function? It matters whether it is painted for a gallery in New York or painted to stand on an altar. I have written an article on the development of the altar painting, which came out in a volume on evolution which unfortunately nobody read.[106] That is a typical example: the development of the altar painting as a genre of art.

I also wrote about the development of landscape painting, how it became a category, a genre of its own.[107] One could go to a dealer and say: I want a landscape for my room to put over the sofa!

Let us take this as an example: many people have written about the development of landscape painting as the expression of a new feeling for nature and the beauty of nature.... I am not sure that a man or a woman in the 14th century going through beautiful scenes really did not enjoy them. But there was no category of landscape painting; that is a very different thing. Later it did become a category of art. You have the same in caricature: there was a moment at the beginning of the 17th century when it became a category of art. I would not say that before that nobody had ever made a picture to make fun of somebody. But you could not say: let's make a caricature of this or that person. There was no word, no genre. And no expectation. In literature, you have similar developments. The most astonishing example is the development of the detective story. Suddenly you get a category where you know exactly what to expect: a murder has been committed; you do not know who committed it, but by the end of the book you will know. In music you have similar fixed categories, such as the dance suite, the fugue, the symphony or sonata.

We come back to the problem: does the artist create a new genre or does he respond to what is expected of him?

There is always a feed-back situation. You can call it dialectic, if you like. Once a particular role for the artist has become accepted by society, it will influence what people expect of art, and their pupils will carry on the tradition.

So you insist on a sociological approach and at the same time on the role played by the individual.

I do not believe in the spirit of the age, in a collective spirit. The artist remains an individual creating something.

You mean you are an individualist when it is a matter of the artist creating new things, but are you equally so when it is a matter of the people looking at his creation?

Yes, both. I mean that we are not entirely determined by the collective. But of course, we are influenced by the collective. You know Daumier said: 'We must follow our own time.' And Ingres said: 'But what if the time is wrong?'

Yes, but then times change, and with them the tastes of the 'consumer'. The wonderful Monet exhibition in London, 'Monet in the 90's', was crowded. But maybe less than a century ago, nobody would have been interested in it?

Of course, there is a lot of pressure on taste. Because one can be taught to discover something.

You told me that beautiful anecdote which happened at that exhibition. It was very crowded and someone recognized you and said: 'It's all your fault.' Do you really think that the art historian has a share in forming fashion?

Up to a point. But I think that much of it goes the other way. I think art historians are influenced by fashions. Just as I told you, I may have been influenced by what Picasso had done when I wrote about Giulio Romano. I think that it quite often happens that art historians become influenced by a contemporary issue without knowing it. Who knows whether I would have written about both representation and decoration if it had not been the time of abstract art when these matters became an issue? They are in the air. One feels that representation has in a way become problematic, and naturally one's interest is directed to this issue.

In fact, I am tempted to believe, it is a suspicion of mine, that exaggerated interest in symbolism and iconology is connected to surrealism. All these 'levels of meaning', and so on, you find it in Max Ernst and Dali. There is always, or nearly always, some sort of link between what art historians do and the taste of the time.

Which means that, however much emphasis you put on the role of the individual, you also think that one has to take account of collective fashions, the tastes of the time.

Yes. Of course. How could one deny the existence of collective fashions? But I have to say that often they are negative. What can easily happen is a kind of social taboo. Certain things are not done. After the triumph of Impressionism, no one who wished to be taken seriously would paint purely photographic or anecdotal pictures. I call this in one of my papers 'the principle of exclusion'. If you accept this exclusion there are many things you can still do, provided you do not do what is now socially taboo, what is considered *passé* and *vieux jeu*. You are then confronted with a new array of possibilities and only those who are really original and inventive can, within these new limitations, create something which becomes accepted, and a fashion. So, the negative is very important in the history of art. For instance, take what we call the International Gothic style, with all these soft curves and glittering gold.... This was an aristocratic style, around 1400. One cannot quite understand it if one cannot also see it as the avoidance of everything angular and hard. Rococo is likewise an avoidance reaction. It does not want to be so heavy and rhetorical as the Baroque. These pairs of contrasts may sound a bit Hegelian. But I do not believe like Hegel that the Absolute Spirit created Rococo. Human beings created it. There is a kind of runaway effect: somebody does something and everything changes because people are tired of the old.

You have often emphasized how important 'snobbery' is in the history of art, the wish to distance oneself from what is judged to be 'facile' or 'vulgar'.

Yes, what Pierre Bourdieu calls *la distinction.*[108] It is immensely important. But, of course, it does not mean that there is no such thing as good art and bad art. There may be a lot of snobbery, but it does not follow that even when you have a very restricted field, you cannot find very interesting solutions and very trivial solutions.

You wrote a long article, republished in 'Ideals and Idols', called 'The Logic of Vanity Fair'.[109] *It expounds your conception of the role of the individual in art, your rejection of Hegelianism (which we have just mentioned), explanations based on 'the spirit of the age' whatever form that might take. Would you say that this summarized your 'philosophy of history'?*

I wrote it for a collective volume on the philosophy of Karl Popper. This 'Logic of Vanity Fair' is an attempt to be more rational than the previous methodological idea about fashions and ages.

The French translator of this article called it 'La logique du jeu de la mode'. What do you think of that?

It is not too bad. It is how I see the changes of fashion and attitudes. That is a Popperian idea: the logic of situation. He actually says, in *The Poverty of Historicism*, that we need more analysis of the logic of situations. His examples are quite simple: if I want to buy a house in Hampstead, I want to buy it as cheaply as possible. But the very fact that I have told the estate agent that I want to buy it has increased the price. That is part of the logic of the situation. In economics you find it all the time: the situation changes through your intervention. If you assume (which is not always true) that everybody acts in his own interest and acts rationally, then everybody has a choice and can calculate, like a chess player, what possibilities exist in any particular situation. Most historians think along these lines in explaining the actions of Napoleon, for instance: they reconstruct what choices were available to him at any particular time.

So the logic of situation is a sort of methodological rule for dealing with historical situations, assuming that people act in their own interest.

But what does it mean for an art historian?

It means that, again, certain possibilities are denied to the artist. Because they have been done before, they are taboo now. And one element in the situation is that he wants to be a success. He wants to make an impression. He is groping his way (not of course consciously) towards something which will be accepted. I sometimes compare it to the growth of a tree. A tree in a wood will always move towards the light. And an artist also develops towards the light, towards people who favour him. He will notice that, unexpectedly perhaps, this or that innovation really makes an impression and he will go on in that direction. I do not want to give the impression that artists are all opportunists. But up to a point everybody wants to please.

I touch on this problem in the introduction to *The Story of Art*, where I quote a letter by Mozart from Paris, where he says: every symphony here starts with a fast movement so I start with a slow introduction. That is part of the logic of the situation: being different and yet acceptable. There is also a limit beyond which it ceases to pay off: if you do something entirely different, it is unintelligible. Of course, there are all the problems which are in the air, and which every artist wishes to solve. For instance, the development of perspective was such a problem, when people started criticizing the earlier art for not being realistic enough. So the artist is always faced with the problem: 'What is there for me to do?'

All this is metaphor, or course. And one cannot go too far. Because there is always something irrational happening in history. You may be completely mad and yet have success. Maybe Hieronymus Bosch was very mad and Philip II of Spain was just mad enough to like his works!

You said just now that all your efforts were devoted to being more rational than previous approaches. In fact, one can say that ever since you chose the profession of art historian you have been, and still are, a fervent rationalist.

Yes, absolutely.

And yet in your biography of Aby Warburg, you say that you do not believe that it is possible to construct a science of art.

No, of course not. What we call science means the exact sciences. History is not an exact science.

But isn't your ambition to be a rationalist in writing the history of art analogous to constructing a science?

Yes, but the ambition has to be reduced. Science makes precise predictions that can be verified or not. We cannot do that in history. We don't predict at all. But what I mean by rationality here is that every statement that we make must have a meaning such that you can also express it in a different form, in a different language. It may not always sound very elegant if I want to translate it into Chinese, but it must be possible to say in

Chinese what I say in English. If you take the writings of my colleagues, particularly the critics or the art historians, many of the things they say are untranslatable, they are metaphors, like poetry. Nothing but emotion. Let me use a figure of speech drawn from banking. The old banknotes always carried the promise that you could exchange them for gold. So with our statements, we ought always to be able to go to the bank and say: give me a fact for it. Therefore I am not very interested in aesthetics or in art criticism, because so much of what these people write is just an expression of their own emotions.

Maybe people do not want to hear rational statements about art. They think that art is an emotional matter.

They are right. It does not worry me if they think so. There are many things we cannot say about art. And the most important thing we cannot say is why something is good or bad. So art criticism is a matter of belief: I believe that Michelangelo is better than Dali. But I cannot prove it. The quality of a work of art is something which is completely embedded in our whole civilization. One cannot isolate it and say: this is why this work is good. That leads nowhere. People have often tried it. If you say: this is good because… let us say, because it is perfectly balanced, you can have another picture which is also perfectly balanced and which is no good at all.

There is no criterion?

There is not one single criterion. You cannot say: this picture is good because it has a diagonal in its composition. It is the same with human beings: too many things come together to make a personality, and too many things come together to make a great Rembrandt. You can go on talking about it for ever.

We went together to see the British Museum exhibition on fakes.[110] *The existence of fakes, and the fact that we have been able to admire them as authentic objects, that even the experts have been taken in, doesn't this complicate the question seriously?*

Well, yes and no. People always wonder how you can admire a fake. But if you think that a picture has been painted by Vermeer, you find it moving. You know that Rembrandt or Vermeer are great masters and when you are shown one of their works you are aroused. But this is not a complete argument for relativism. In many respects, our civilization conditions us to be enthusiastic and to admire things. But this does not mean that we do not really admire them. If somebody tells you that Raphael is wonderful, you try to make yourself like him, little by little, but at the same time you do really discover him. How could you ever discover him otherwise?

You know that I do not believe in the innocent eye. If somebody brings me a painting and says: my twelve-year-old son painted this, my attitude will be very different from what it would be if they said Albrecht Dürer painted it. I cannot help it. One would be inhuman if one did not react to what one knows is worthy af attention. We come back to the problem of Romanticism and sincerity. We are never quite sincere in that sense because we are never isolated. This is an important feeling. Religious emotions are collective. Up to a point art is also a religion.

In your volume called 'Ideals and Idols', you put the emphasis on the reality of values. We can know that a great master is a great master. But all these things that we have been discussing - rediscoveries in the history of art, changes in taste, etc. - all this makes me wonder. When we read Francis Haskell's book on 'rediscoveries' in art,[111] *which is all about how people suddenly start admiring this or that painter who was previously despised or ignored, one has to doubt the objective 'reality' of values.*

You are absolutely right. Haskell has written an excellent book. I have reviewed it, and I said: I agree with everything except his relativism.[112] Titian would be a great master even if the time should come when nobody wants to look at his paintings. He will always remain the best of his time. That is partly a technical and a psychological matter. What does great mean? You can even call an acrobat or a football player great. I do not think one can be a complete relativist in art. But I do not think that there can be a rational, scientific criterion by which you can say: this is really the best.

The reason why I think that there is a limit to our rational understanding of what is great art is quite simple: I believe in the fundamentally biological foundation of our reactions. If you like, that links me with psychoanalysis. I do believe that a great work of art strikes a subtle balance between what seems too obvious and what seems too difficult. I know of no better discussion of this problem than one that I found in Cicero, in his treatise *De Oratore*. I have already quoted this passage elsewhere, but I should like to quote it again. It describes the limits – which orators must always bear in mind – of the pleasure of the senses:

> For it is hard to say why exactly it is that the things which most strongly gratify our senses and excite them most vigorously at their first appearance, are the ones from which we are most speedily estranged by a feeling of disgust and satiety. How much more brilliant, as a rule, in beauty and variety of colouring are the contents of new pictures than those of old ones! and nevertheless the new ones, though they captivated us at first sight, later on fail to give us pleasure – although it is also true that in the case of old pictures the actual roughness and old-fashioned style are an attraction. In singing, how much more delightful and charming are trills and flourishes than notes firmly held! and yet the

> former meet with protest not only from persons of severe taste but, if used too often, even from the general public. This may be observed in the case of the rest of the senses – that perfumes compounded with an extremely sweet and penetrating scent do not give us pleasure for so long as those that are moderately fragrant, and a thing that seems to have the scent of earth is more esteemed than one that suggests saffron; and that in touch itself there are degrees of softness and smoothness. Taste is the most voluptuous of all the senses and more sensitive to sweetness than the rest, yet how quickly even it dislikes and rejects anything extremely sweet! Who can go on taking a sweet drink or food for a long time? whereas in both classes things that pleasurably affect the sense in a moderate degree most easily escape causing satiety. Thus in all things the greatest pleasures are only narrowly separated from disgust.[113]

What Cicero is analysing is precisely the complex relation between immediate satisfaction and aesthetic pleasure. There are impressions that bring immediate satisfaction to the senses, for example those that have charm, brilliance or simple musical rhythms. But it is also a psychological fact that immediate satisfaction can lead to disgust. A psychoanalyst would perhaps say that we learn to deny ourselves this satisfaction in favour of more sublimated pleasures. I think that without these basic reactions art could not exist, but one cannot explain art wholly in terms of these reactions; one must also take account of our self-denials. This is what I mean when I talk of balance. It is evident that the exact point of balance will differ according to individual people, civilizations, epochs and social conditions. That is why I find Bourdieu's researches so interesting. He has shown that certain sections of the population look for immediate, simple satisfactions, while the intellectuals take pride in rejecting kitsch and deny themselves these simple pleasures. Where I differ from Bourdieu is that I do not think that this important distinction leads inevitably to absolute aesthetic relativism.

I believe that the two elements that I have mentioned are quite real, and you could take one of Beethoven's late quartets as an example of the process by which the simple elements of melodies and attractive rhythms are sublimated and integrated into a much larger context which demands a certain experience and effort to understand and appreciate.

What you are proposing is almost a 'psychology of aesthetic perception'?

Yes. If you give a deaf person the score of a piece by Bach or Mozart, he can learn to see the composition of themes and their recurrence but not why this is so marvellous because he cannot feel it. And this feeling is biological. Take rhythm: we certainly react to rhythmical movements and sounds, and this biological reaction is universal. But the music of India and the music of Europe have both modified this simple reaction. The difference between the monotonous beat of pop music and the rhythmical architecture of a great symphony is precisely that in classical music the primitive reaction is delayed and denied for a more varied satisfaction. It is the same with our reaction to colours or forms.

I attach great importance to these observations because there is a fashion now in the humanities to deny that the old notion of human nature still has any utility. I consider this tendency to be dangerous because it undermines the great 18th-century idea of the unity of mankind, an idea that is so menaced anyway by racism and other movements of the same sort. When I received an unexpected invitation, I don't know how, to deliver the opening address of an important conference on Germanic studies at Göttingen dedicated to 'Controversies ancient and modern', I chose to raise this issue, which seemed so crucial to me. I contrasted two quotations: an epigram of Goethe, saying that through reading Plutarch he learned that we were all human beings, and a passage from Hegel denying that we can ever understand the men of classical Antiquity because they represent a different stage in the evolution of the human mind. In this address I also criticized the fashion of 'deconstruction', and I argued that we can effectively understand the cultures of alien peoples and remote epochs, although, naturally, we can also misunderstand them.[114]

Since then I have continued in several pieces of writing to oppose extreme relativism. In a lecture that I gave in Rome I tried to show that in spite of what Thomas Kuhn says (which has been much exaggerated by his followers), you cannot write the history of any branch of knowledge, whatever it may be, from a completely relativist point of view. No one can deny that thanks to Champollion and a few others we have succeeded in reading Egyptian hieroglyphics and that we know, in most cases, what they mean.

Similarly, I have written against the idea that the interpretation of works of art can be completely subjective. We *know* that the picture by Rembrandt known as *The Night Watch* is not a night watch, but a scene taking place in full daylight.

All these texts are published in my most recent collection called *Topics of Our Time*.[115]

But is there not a contradiction between being so fiercely hostile to relativism in history and aesthetics and at the same time asserting that there are no objective criteria for deciding whether a work is good or bad? And above all, as you know better than anybody, the 'biology of aesthetic pleasure', which you have just explained, has to take account of differences between epochs, civilizations and, obviously, within the same society, between individuals.

Our reactions in front of a work of art are simply too complex to be analysed scientifically. I think, for instance, that it is vain and quite pointless to try to enumerate all the elements that come together in our preference for this or that artist or poet. We react as members of our civilization who have absorbed its values through our education and society. I have explained that some of these values are purely biological, including perhaps eroticism, to which psychoanalysis attaches so much importance. But others belong to the sphere that psychoanalysis calls the 'superego', such as ideas of nobility, or heroism or tenderness. Or generosity or the sublime. Or even love, insofar as it is distinguished from sexuality. These values enter into all our sensations, into our reactions when we admire a picture by Raphael or Michelangelo, when we read Shakespeare or listen to Mozart. There, again, it is a question of reaction and self-denial. But in our society the self-denial of which I speak has a moral dimension which is not strongly recognized in all civilizations.

*   *   *

What are you working on now? You have several times mentioned your current project on 'The Preference for the Primitive'....

I have become very interested in the question of the taste for the primitive. I gave three lectures on it in Princeton, which became five lectures in Los Angeles. I have said before that many people interpreted *Art and Illusion*, which studied the development of naturalism, as if I meant that art gets better and better the more naturalistic it becomes. So I am now writing about the reaction against naturalism, the idea, often advanced during the centuries, that too much naturalism leads to decadence and corruption, and that one must go back to early beginnings, to primitives. You will see that this choice of subject is not unconnected with the way my book was misinterpreted. But it is also connected with my earliest themes. Before I left school, you remember, I wrote this long dissertation about changes in the approach to art.

But in addition to that, I suppose that you continue to work on a thousand other matters?

I recently wrote something about the Romanesque style. Somebody who paid for the restoration of an old church on the Lago Maggiore invited me to talk about the Romanesque and that church. I said that I knew nothing about Romanesque churches. When he seemed very disappointed, I said: I cannot talk about Romanesque churches but I can talk about the rediscovery of the Romanesque style. I did give a talk about this which has now been published in Italian.[116] That is part of my more general interest in taste.

Among my other recent things, I could also mention the educational films produced as cassettes, for the Getty Foundation, in which I analyse the effects of light in paintings. These films were made here, at home: I describe very simply the effects of light on domestic objects and compare this with the effects of light in pictures in the National Gallery. I think it is quite entertaining. In the introduction to these films I say that some critics might call this approach a bit philistine and accuse me of ignoring the artistic revolutions of the 20th century. But, in the first place, I am a historian, not a critic of art; and in the second, even the revolutions of our century (which interest me a great deal) derive their significance from their remoteness from pictorial naturalism.

You told me about a project that you had for a book, or a study, which you would write with the artist of this portrait, hanging in your room, which shows you surrounded by books and papers.

Yes, one of my American friends, Stanley Meltzoff. He was originally an art historian, a pupil of Panofsky. He wrote some important articles on the reputation of the Le Nain brothers and other artists. He later became an art teacher and illustrator, and as he had all his life been a passionate diver, he became an expert in marine life and specialized in painting pictures of fish in the water. I corresponded with him for many years because he took a great interest in theoretical questions. When he showed me a commentary on his methods as a painter of nature, I proposed that we should join forces. I wanted to continue the line of research represented by *Art and Illusion* and explore, in more concrete detail, how the great masters achieved their effects of light and texture.

Whatever comes of this project, it does seem to me very important to draw the art historians' attention to these technical questions. I really have the impression that nowadays they write about everything except about art. We read studies about women, about blacks, about the art market... I certainly don't deny that these questions can present a certain interest, but after all one may surely ask of the history of art that it concern itself with art! Because I think that we still know too little. In fact I should like to say to my colleagues that we still don't have a history of art.

EPILOGUE

When you look at a picture, can you forget that you are a professional, and see it as something more than an object of study or a series of problems and enigmas to be solved?

Frankly, I find the question strange. I hope and believe that I have never lost my enjoyment of great works of art through my intellectual interests. On the contrary, I may have learned to enjoy certain paintings more through my interests. I have sometimes suspected that my enjoyment of classical music is more spontaneous and natural than my love of the visual arts. I don't want to exaggerate, of course. I think I can enjoy the masterpieces of Greek sculpture, of medieval goldsmith work or of Titian and Rembrandt with equal spontaneity, but maybe I began my theoretical interest in art history hoping that I would gain in enjoyment and understanding. I believe I was right in that my enjoyment has profited by my work. What is more, the success of my book *The Story of Art* indicates to me that I also succeeded in helping others to such enjoyment. I might never have been able to do this for music!

But the fact of your having devoted so much time and so much labour to the rational study of art and works of art, doesn't all that interfere somewhat with the emotion that you feel in front of a masterpiece?

No. On the contrary, you learn to see better. And to admire the great artists even more. It is some consolation for growing old: I marvel more and more at the incredible delicacy with which Chardin paints some perfectly simple thing, like strawberries in a dish.

In your biography of Aby Warburg, you wrote: 'He never saw himself as a detached observer.' Can we apply this sentence to you? I have the feeling that you consider the art historian to be what we call in France 'un intellectuel engagé'.

Yes. You are right.

You are fighting for values?

Yes, that is how I see the art historian, or the historian.

And what are the values you are fighting for?

I think I can say this very simply: the traditional civilization of Western Europe. I know there are also very horrible things in that civilization. I know it very well. But I think art historians are the spokesmen of our civilization: we want to know more about our Olympus.

In order to preserve the memory of the past?

Not only the memory, but also what we owe. I have criticized those who talk of 'escapism'. Life would be unbearable if we could never escape to the consolations of great art. One must pity those who lack contact with this heritage of the past. One must be so grateful that one can listen to Mozart and look at Velazquez and must be sorry for those who cannot.

NOTES

BIBLIOGRAPHY

INDEX

ACKNOWLEDGMENTS

NOTES

1 The Leverhulme Lecture of 1981, reprinted in *Tributes*, Oxford, 1984, pp. 71-92.

2 These letters have been published. See 'Zwei Briefe Hofmannsthals an Karl Gombrich' in *Hofmannsthal Blätter*, 17/18, 1977, pp. 295-296.

3 Peter Gay, *Freud. A Life*, London and New York, 1988.

4 *Gastspiele*, Vienna, 1992.

5 See Adolf Busch, *Briefe. Bilder. Erinnerungen*, ed. Irene Serkin-Busch, with a preface by E.H. Gombrich, Walpole, New Hampshire, Arts and Letters Press, 1991. There is also an English language edition.

6 *Vienne 1880-1938. La Joyeuse Apocalypse*, an exhibition held at the Centre Pompidou, Paris, at the beginning of 1986; the Catalogue, by Jean Clair, Paris, Editions du Centre Georges Pompidou, 1986.

7 *Die Kunstliteratur*, Vienna, 1924. In the Italian editions of 1935, 1956, 1967 the bibliography is brought up to date by Otto Kurz.

8 Cf. E. H. Gombrich, 'The Exploration of Culture Contacts. The Services to Scholarship of Otto Kurz (1908-1975)' in *Tributes. Interpreters of our Cultural Tradition*, Oxford, Phaidon Press, 1984, pp. 235-249.

9 'Zum Werke Giulio Romanos', *Jahrbuch der Kunsthistorischen Sammlungen Wien*, N.F.8. pp. 79-104 (1934) and N.F.9. pp. 121-150 (1935).

10 *Eine Kurze Weltgeschichte für junge Leser*, Du Mont Verlag, Cologne, 1985 with an additional Chapter.

11 Cf. E. H. Gombrich, 'The Study of Art and the Study of Man. Reminiscences of Collaboration with Ernst Kris (1900-1957)' in *Tributes* 1984, pp. 221-223.

12 'Eine Verkannte Karolingische Pyxis im Wiener Kunsthistorischen Museum' in *Jahrbuch der Kunsthistorischen Sammlungen in Wien*, N. F., 7, 1933, pp. 1-14.

13 'Die Charakterköpfe des Franz Xavier Messerschmidt' in *Jahrbuch der Kunsthistorischen Sammlungen in Wien*, 1932. pp 169-228.

14 Ernst Kris and Otto Kurz, *'Legend, Myth and Magic in the Image of the Artist'*, Yale University Press 1979 with a Preface by E.H. Gombrich.

15 For the history of the Warburg Library, see the memoir by Fritz Saxl in my *Aby Warburg*, London 1970, pp. 325-338.

16 E.H. Gombrich and Ernst Kris, 'The Principles of Caricature' in *British Journal of Medical Psychology*, XVII, 1938, pp. 319-342. Reprinted in Ernst Kris, *Psychoanalytic Explorations in Art*, New York, 1952.

17 E. H. Gombrich and Ernst Kris, *Caricature*, Harmondsworth, 1940.

18 My own second thoughts (and

those of Ernst Kris) can be found in my lecture 'Magic, Myth and Metaphor, Reflections on Pictorial Satire', in XXVII *Congrès International d'histoire de l'art, 1989, Actes I*, Strasbourg, 1990, pp. 23-66.

19 In *Art and Illusion*, Chapter 9: 'The Experiment of Caricature', Oxford, Phaidon Press, 1966, pp. 279-303.

20 Only two volumes had been published in Germany before the Institute went into exile.

21 *Aby Warburg, an Intellectual Biography*, London, the Warburg Institute, 1970.

22 'The Subject of Poussin's *Orion*' in *Symbolic Images*, London, Phaidon Press, 1972, pp. 119-122.

23 This exchange of letters in the form of Latin poems was published privately by the Friends' Press, the Fitzwilliam Museum, Cambridge, December 1984, under the title: *The Warburg Institute and H.M Office of Works.*

24 See Olive Renier and Vladimir Rubinstein, *Assigned to Listen, The Evesham Experience, 1939-43*, London, British Broadcasting Corporation, 1986.

25 'Spracherlebnisse', in *Die Presse* (Vienna), 14/15 May, 1988. Reprinted in *Gastspiele,* Vienna, 1992.

26 'Myth and Reality in German Wartime Broadcasts', in *Ideals and Idols*, Oxford, Phaidon Press, 1979, pp. 93-111.

27 *Burlington Magazine*, 84, 1944. See Note 22.

28 The genesis of the book is described in my article in the *Independent* of 6 Jan 1990 under the title 'Old Masters and Other Household Goods'.

29 E. H. Gombrich, 'The Warburg Institute. A Personal Memoir', in *The Art Newspaper*, No. 2, November 1990.

30 'Stilgeschichte und Sprachgeschichte der bildenden Kunst' in *Sitzungsberichte der Bayerischen Akademie der Wissenschaften*, 1935/I. p. 10.

31 Hans Belting, *Bild und Kult, Eine Geschichte der Bilder vor dem Zeitalter der Kunst*, Munich, 1990

32 'Art-as-such. The Sociology of Modern Aesthetics', and 'From Addison to Kant. Modern Aesthetics and the Exemplary Art', in *Doing Things with Texts. Essays in Criticism and Critical Theory*, ed. Michael Fischer, New York and London, W. W. Norton, 1989 pp. 135-187.

33 See my preface to the catalogue *Leonardo da Vinci*, Hayward Gallery, 1989, pp. 1-4.

34 *Art and Illusion*, pp. 99-125.

35 *L'Art religieux de la fin du Moyen Age en France*, Paris, Albin Michel, 1908.

36 E. H. Gombrich, 'Giotto's Portrait of Dante', in *New Light on Old Masters. Studies in the Art of the Renaissance.* IV, Oxford, Phaidon Press, 1986, pp.11-31.

37 *Doing Things with Texts ... op. cit.* See Note 32.

38 *The Poverty of Historicism, Economica* 11, 12, 1944/45, London, Routledge and Kegan Paul and Boston, Beacon Press, 1957.

39 'Demand and Supply in the History of Styles: the Example of International Gothic', in *Three Cultures,* symposium organized by the Praemium Erasmianum Foundation, ed. M. Bal, A. B. Mitzman and J. Stumpel, Rotterdam, 1989, pp. 127-159.

40 'The Necessity of Tradition. An Interpretation of the Poetics of I.A. Richards (1895-1979), in *Tributes.* See Note 8.

41 See Note 24. A memorandum by me is quoted on pp.75-79.

42 The three works by Gibson to

which I refer most frequently are: *The Perception of the Visual World*, Cambridge Mass., The Riverside Press, 1950; *The Senses Considered as Perceptual Systems*, Boston, Houghton Mifflin Company, 1966; and *The Ecological Approach to Perception*, Boston, Houghton Mifflin Company, 1979.

43 See for example the letters formed by shadows, in *Art and Illusion*, p. 263, and above all the so called 'Kanisza triangle' in *The Sense of Order*, p. 107.

44 *Illusion in Nature and Art*, London, Duckworth, 1973. p. 211.

45 Prof. D. G. Ross, in *Science*, Vol 241, January 1989, pp. 234-236.

46 *Art and Illusion*, p. 278.

47 *Die Spätrömische Kunstindustrie*, Vienna, 1901.

48 *Die Naturwiedergabe in der älteren griechischen Kunst*, Rome, 1900.

49 *Die Kunst des Mittelalters*, Berlin - Neubabelsberg, 1923.

50 *The Elements of Drawing*, London, 1843.

51 'Voir la nature, voir les peintures', in *Les Cahiers du musée national d'Art moderne*, Paris, Centre Georges Pompidou, No. 24, Summer 1988, pp. 21-43.

52 Cited from Voltaire's *Physique newtonienne* in my lecture referred to in Note 51.

53 *Monet in the '90s. The Series Paintings.* Exhibition shown in London in the Autumn of 1990. The Catalogue, edited by Paul Hayes Tucker, was published by the Museum of Fine Arts, Boston, and Yale University Press, 1989.

54 *The Image and the Eye. Further Studies in the Psychology of Pictorial Representation*, Oxford, Phaidon Press, 1982.

55 For reference see my Chapter 'Plato in Modern Dress' in *Topics of our Time*, London 1991, Note 26.

56 See the article by J. J. Gibson. 'The Information Available in Pictures', in *Leonardo*, IV, 1971, pp. 27-35. My reply, *ibid*, pp. 195-197. Then Gibson again, *ibid*, pp. 197-199. And finally my last reply, *ibid*, p. 308.

57 *Ibid.* p. 196.

58 I quote this letter in my review of Eduard S. Reed's book, *J. J. Gibson and the Psychology of Perception*, in *New York Review of Books*, January 19, 1985, pp. 13-15.

59 Exhibition held in the Grand Palais, Paris, in 1979; catalogue by Pierre Rosenberg.

60 Nelson Goodman, *Languages of Art. An Approach to a Theory of Symbols*, New York, 1968.

61 'The "What" and the "How": Perspective Representation and the Phenomenal World', in *Logic and Art: Essays in Honor of Nelson Goodman*, ed. R. Rudner and I. Sheffler, New York, 1972.

62 *The Image and the Eye*, p. 284.

63 'Pictures in the Mind?' in *Images and Understanding*, edited by Horace Barlow and others, Cambridge, 1990, pp. 358-364.

64 'Art and Self-Transcendence' in *Ideals and Idols*, Oxford, 1979, p. 130.

65 *Cognitive Psychology*, New York, Appleton Century Crofts, 1967.

66 *Illusion in Nature and Art.* See Note 44.

67 *The Image and the Eye.* See Note 54.

68 See 'In Search of Cultural History' in *Ideals and Idols*, pp. 25-29, and 'The Father of Art History'. A Reading of the *Lectures on Aesthetics* of G. W. F. Hegel (1770-1831), in *Tributes*, pp. 51-96. See Note 8.

69 *The Sense of Order*, p. 1. The quotation is taken from Karl Popper's *Objective*

Knowledge; An Evolutionary Approach, Oxford, Clarendon Press, 1972.
70 *Reflections on the History of Art. Views and Reviews*, Col. Richard Woodfield. Oxford, Phaidon Press, 1987.
71 Cambridge (Mass.) and London, 1957.
72 'Meditations on a Hobby Horse or the Roots of Artistic Form', reprinted in E. H. Gombrich, *Meditations on a Hobby Horse and Other Essays on the Theory of Art*, London, Phaidon Press, 1963, pp. 1-11.
73 See 'Conversation au coin du feu entre Karl Popper et Konrad Lorenz', in Konrad Lorenz and Karl Popper, *L'Avenir est ouvert*, Paris, Flammarion, 1990. Originally published in Vienna.
74 In 'Essay sur l'architecture religieuse du moyen âge', Paris 1837, reprinted in *Etudes sur les arts du Moyen Age* (edited by Pierre Josserand), Paris, 1967.
75 E. H. Gombrich, *The Sense of Order*, pp. 213-214. Also *Styles of Art and Styles of Life*, The Reynolds Lecture, 1990, Royal Academy of Arts, London, 1991.
76 'In Search of Cultural History', in *Ideals and Idols*, pp. 24-59.
77 *Gothic Architecture and Scholasticism*, Latrobe, Pa., 1951.
78 Stockholm, 1960.
79 On George Boas, see E. H. Gombrich, 'The History of Ideas. A Personal Tribute to George Boas', in *Tributes*, pp. 165-183.
80 *Renaissance and Renascences*, Stockholm, 1960, p. 3, Note 1.
81 '*Idea* in the Theory of Art: Philosophy or Rhetoric?' in *Idea, VI, Colloquio Internazionale*, Rome 5-7, January 1989. *Atti a cura di M. Fattori e M. L. Bianchi*, Rome, Edizione dell'Ateneo, 1991, pp. 411-420.
82 *Tributes*, pp. 51-69.
83 June 1968, pp. 356-360.
84 'Raphael's *Stanza della Segnatura* and the Nature of its Symbolism', in *Symbolic Images*, pp. 85-101.
85 'As it was in the Days of Noe', in *The Heritage of Apelles. Studies in the Art of the Renaissance*, Oxford, Phaidon Press, 1976, pp. 83-90.
86 E. H. Gombrich, 'The *Sala dei Venti* in the Palazzo del Tè', in *Symbolic Images*, pp. 109-118.
87 See Note 22.
88 'Raphael's *Madonna della sedia*', in *The Heritage of Apelles*, pp. 64-80.
89 'Leonardo and the Magicians: Polemics and Rivalry', in *New Light on Old Masters. Studies in the Art of the Renaissance*, pp. 61-88.
90 *Norm and Form*, *Symbolic Images*, *The Heritage of Apelles* and *New Light on Old Masters.*
91 See my article with Caroline Elam, 'Lorenzo de' Medici and a Frustrated Villa Project at Vallombrosa', in *Florence and Italy, Renaissance Studies in Honour of Nicolai Rubinstein*, Westfield College, University of London, 1988, pp. 481-492.
92 'Botticelli's Mythologies. A Study in the Neo-Platonic Symbolism of his Circle', in *Symbolic Images*, pp. 36-81.
93 'A Postscript as a Preface', *Symbolic Images*, pp. 31-35.
94 *Marsile Ficin et l'art*, 1957.
95 In *Symbolic Images*, pp. 123-191.
96 *The Divine Comedy. Paradiso*, Canto IV, lines 40-47, Translation Gombrich.
97 See Note 81.
98 *Symbolic Images*, pp. 1-22.
99 E. H. Gombrich, 'Sull'iconographia degli affreschi del Correggio nella Camera di San Paolo', in *Il Monastero di San Paolo*, ed. Marzio dall'Acqua, Cassa di Risparmio di Parma, Franco Maria Ricci, 1990.

100 *The Art of Describing. Dutch Art in the XVIIth Century*, New Haven and London, 1983.
101 New York, 1953.
102 *In Styles of Art and Styles of Life*. See Note 75.
103 See my Freud memorial lecture in *Tributes*, p. 94.
104 *The Heritage of Apelles*, pp. 93-110.
105 The letter (by Lorenzo Leonbruno) is quoted in my *New Light on old Masters*, Oxford, 1986, p. 149.
106 'Evolution in the Arts: the Altar Painting, its Ancestry and Progress', in *Evolution and its Influence*, ed. Alan Grafen, Oxford, Clarendon Press, 1989, pp. 105-125.
107 'Renaissance Artistic Theory and the Rise of Landscape', in *Norm and Form*, pp. 107-121.
108 *La Distinction. Critique sociale du jugement*, Paris, Editions de Minuit, 1979.
109 'The Logic of Vanity Fair. Historicism in the Study of Fashion. Style and Taste', in *Ideals and Idols*, pp. 60-92.
110 *Fake? The Art of Deception*, exhibition held at the British Museum from March to September 1990; catalogue by Mark Jones, London, British Museum Publications, 1990.
111 *Rediscoveries in Art. Some Aspects of Taste, Fashion and Collection in England and France*, Oxford, Phaidon Press, 1976.
112 'The Whirligig of Taste', in *Reflections on the History of Art, Views and Reviews*, ed. Richard Woodfield, 1987, pp. 163-167.
113 *De Oratore*, translated by H. Rackham, Loeb Classical Library, 1940.
114 '... "Sind eben alles Menschen gewesen." Zum Kulturrelativismus in den Geisteswissenschaften', in *Kontroversen, alte und neue*, Akten des VII. Internationalen Germanisten Kongresses, Göttingen, 1985. Tübingen, Niemeyer Verlag, 1986, pp. 17-25. English in *Topics of our Time*, Phaidon Press, London, 1991, pp. 36-46.
115 Phaidon Press, London, 1991.
116 *Dall'archeologia alla storia dell'arte: Tappe della fortuna critica dello stile romanico*, Turin, Einaudi, 1990.

A SELECT BIBLIOGRAPHY

BOOKS

The Story of Art, London, Phaidon Press, 1950. Fifteenth edition, revised and expanded, 1989.

Art and Illusion. A Study in the Psychology of Pictorial Representation, London, Phaidon Press, 1960.

Meditations on a Hobby Horse and Other Essays on the Theory of Art, London, Phaidon Press, 1963.

Norm and Form. Studies in the Art of the Renaissance I, London, Phaidon Press, 1966.

Aby Warburg. An Intellectual Biography, London, The Warburg Institute, University of London, 1970.

Symbolic Images. Studies in the Art of the Renaissance II, London, Phaidon Press, 1972.

The Heritage of Apelles. Studies in the Art of the Renaissance III, Oxford, Phaidon Press, 1976.

Means and Ends, The Walter Neurath Memorial lecture, London, Thames and Hudson, 1976.

The Sense of Order. A Study in the Psychology of Decorative Art, Oxford, Phaidon Press, 1979.

Ideals and Idols. Essays on Values in History and in Art, Oxford, Phaidon Press, 1979.

The Image and the Eye. Further Studies in the Psychology of Pictorial Representation, Oxford, Phaidon Press, 1982.

Tributes. Interpreters of Our Cultural Tradition, Oxford, Phaidon Press, 1984.

New Light on Old Masters. Studies in the Art of the Renaissance IV, Oxford, Phaidon Press, 1986.

Reflections on the History of Art. Views and Reviews, (ed. Richard Woodfield) Oxford, Phaidon Press, 1987.

Topics of our Time, Twentieth Century Issues in Learning and in Art, London, Phaidon Press, 1991.

BOOKS WRITTEN IN COLLABORATION

Caricature (with Ernst Kris), London, Penguin Books, 1940.

Illusion in Nature and Art (with Richard Gregory), London, Duckworth, 1973.

CRITICAL STUDIES

Carlos Montes Serrano, *Creatividad y Estilo. El concepto de estilo en E.H. Gombrich*, Universidad de Navarra, 1989.

Joaquín Lorda Iñarra, *Gombrich: Una Teoria del Arte*. Barcelona, Ediciones Internacionales Universitarias 1991.

Martina Sitt (ed.), *Kunsthistoriker in eigener Sache*, Berlin, Dietrich Reimer, 1990 (pp. 63–100).

Klaus Lepsky, *Ernst H. Gombrich, Theorie und Methode*. Vienna and Cologne, Böhlau 1991.

INDEX

PHOTOGRAPHIC ACKNOWLEDGMENTS

Cornell University (photograph by Russell C. Hamilton): page 91; Pino Guidolotti: pp. 89, 95; Emil Paul Dobson: p. 96; Jerry Bauer: p. 93.